**Elements in Religion and Monotheism**
edited by
Paul K. Moser
*Loyola University Chicago*
Chad Meister
*Affiliate Scholar, Ansari Institute for Global Engagement with Religion, University of Notre Dame*



# MONOTHEISM AND WISDOM IN THE HEBREW BIBLE

## *An Uneasy Pair?*

James L. Crenshaw
*Robert L. Flowers Emeritus Professor of Old Testament*
*Duke University*

Shaftesbury Road, Cambridge CB2 8EA, United Kingdom

One Liberty Plaza, 20th Floor, New York, NY 10006, USA

477 Williamstown Road, Port Melbourne, VIC 3207, Australia

314–321, 3rd Floor, Plot 3, Splendor Forum, Jasola District Centre, New Delhi – 110025, India

103 Penang Road, #05-06/07, Visioncrest Commercial, Singapore 238467

Cambridge University Press is part of Cambridge University Press & Assessment, a department of the University of Cambridge.

We share the University's mission to contribute to society through the pursuit of education, learning and research at the highest international levels of excellence.

www.cambridge.org
Information on this title: www.cambridge.org/9781009491877

DOI: 10.1017/9781009491914



When citing this work, please include a reference to the DOI 10.1017/9781009491914

First published 2025

*A catalogue record for this publication is available from the British Library*

ISBN 978-1-009-49187-7 Hardback
ISBN 978-1-009-49189-1 Paperback
ISSN 2631-3014 (online)
ISSN 2631-3006 (print)

# Monotheism and Wisdom in the Hebrew Bible

## An Uneasy Pair?

Elements in Religion and Monotheism

DOI: 10.1017/9781009491914
First published online: January 2025

---

James L. Crenshaw
*Duke University*

**Author for correspondence:** James L. Crenshaw, jameslcrenshaw@comcast.net

**Abstract:** Monotheism, belief in only one God, and wisdom, learning to cope by reason alone and teaching others to do so, faced resistance in the polytheistic world of ancient Egypt, Mesopotamia, and lesser states including Israel. Paradoxically, in early biblical wisdom (Proverbs, Job, and Ecclesiastes) the deity was thought to be both human-like, with disturbing attributes, and increasingly transcendent – silent, disembodied, and inactive. Like Egyptian Ma'at, God the creator established the universe by decree, a law rewarding goodness and punishing evil, the flaw in creation, never satisfactorily resolved. Satan, a semidivine rival, bore responsibility for bad things, while Wisdom, a personified female, communicated God's will to the discerning. Combining biblical revelation and Hellenism, Sirach and Wisdom of Solomon chose piety over Job's realism and the vanity literature of Ecclesiastes. Over millennia, the concept of God evolved, continuing a process begun in Paleolithic times.

**Keywords:** wisdom, dualism, act/consequence, personification, monotheism



ISBNs: 9781009491877 (HB), 9781009491891 (PB), 9781009491914 (OC)
ISSNs: 2631-3014 (online), 2631-3006 (print)

# Contents

## Introduction: One God or Many Gods?

Monotheism, the belief in only one God and the claim that all other gods were an illusion, and wisdom, coping with everyday life by reason alone, are difficult to reconcile. Founded on three pillars (revelation, law, and restoration), monotheism is the product of fear and conflict, fear of the unknown and a desire to erect boundaries between the known and the unknown. Wisdom makes no claim to possess privileged knowledge beyond that subject to objective verification. Whereas monotheism divides humanity, at least in its three Abrahamic representatives, wisdom views humankind as a single family. Emerging as a response to the social and political instabilities in which a small set of Judean communities found themselves, monotheism was "fashioned in the fires of political struggle," giving voice to those on the margins of power who sought the restoration of the kingdom and political authority.[1]

For many readers, monotheism suggests the belief in only one God, whereas wisdom implies a deep intellectual understanding believed to have been acquired by only a few people who reap the benefits of advanced age and wide experience.[2] For our purposes, however, wisdom is short for wisdom literature, a special area of research under a broader discipline, religious studies.[3] The term wisdom literature originated to describe texts in the Hebrew Bible (Old Testament) that offer urgent advice to youth on how to succeed in life and ask probing questions of everyone about the problem of unjust suffering and the meaning of existence. The word "wisdom" appears throughout these texts and is even personified as a divine emanation or avatar.

---

[1] See the stimulating discussion by Jeremiah W. Cataldo, *A Social-Political History of Monotheism: From Judah to the Byzantines* (London: Routledge, 2018). The quoted phrase is from p. 225. See also Mark S. Smith, *God in Translation: Deities in Cross-Cultural Discourse in the Biblical World* (Grand Rapids, MI: Eerdmans, 2010), especially pp. 178–180 where he argues that Israel's monotheism emerged in the context of its lack of power in the face of empires, perhaps as a form of resistance to them.

[2] From inception, biblical monotheism was an aspirational ideal, like moral perfection. It competed with belief in many gods, which continued in remote areas where the appeal of Asherah compensated for portrayal of YHWH as Israel's husband. The emergence of a female personification of Wisdom supports archaeological evidence of longing for a mother goddess. Monotheism tended to elevate YHWH (the eventual victor in the hunt for a name among many—El, El Shaddai, Elyon, Baal, etc.) for the biblical deity, creating distance from devotees, spatially and emotionally. Moreover, a single God had to assume responsibility for bad things that inevitably occurred. Tribal deities were believed to have been more personally involved with humans. To them, women prayed for fertility, men for victory in battle, everyone for health. The origin of monotheism, which others have explored in great depth, lies outside my task.

[3] The study of wisdom literature came of age with the publication of Gerhard von Rad, *Weisheit in Israel* (Neukirchen-Vluyn: Neukirchener Verlag, 1970). An English translation soon followed. For a critique, see James L. Crenshaw, "Wisdom in Israel by Gerhard von Rad," *Religious Studies Review* 2 (1976), 6–12, and for an analysis of each book in the wisdom corpus and ancient Near Eastern parallels, see James L. Crenshaw, *Old Testament Wisdom: An Introduction*. 3rd ed. (Louisville, KY: Westminster John Knox, 2010).

Belief in God is as old as Paleolithic times. Insufficient evidence prevents us from saying whether it arose as monotheism, the worship of the sun, its earliest manifestation in Egypt, or polytheism with gods like Inana in Sumer, Ishtar in Babylon, Anat in Canaan, Isis in Egypt, and Aphrodite in Greece. Nor do we know whether religion began as an epiphany of wonder as Rudolf Otto believed, or as fear, a feeling of absolute dependence, as Friedrich Schleiermacher imagined. Ancient Near Eastern history seems to suggest an early polytheism, broken briefly in Egypt in the fourteenth century BCE, and superseded during the Axial Age, a period characterized by a merchant economy and vast wealth. The emerging monotheism has survived in the West despite Christian theologians' introduction of Trinitarian thought, the Enlightenment, secular humanism, atheism, and the death of God theology. It is too early to say whether the violence of the Abrahamic religions and their fundamentalism that manifests itself in political activism will put an end to theism as we know it today. Monotheism has always had inherent dangers, the disappearing deity in transcendence and its opposite, the humanizing of God. In addition, polytheism appealed to the masses who resisted royal and priestly enforcement of loyalty to them and their deity. A third alternative, the loss of self in the paradox, All or Nothing, has always claimed a few followers in India and in Judaism, Christianity, and Islam.

Those for whom the Bible does more than gather dust on a coffee table may recognize the books called wisdom literature in the description above, for Proverbs abounds in parental counsel made urgent by the consequences of decisions by the young, the book of Job agonizes over innocent suffering and how to speak to and about God when assurances of faith are believed to be unreliable. Ecclesiastes (also known as Qoheleth) views life as *hebel* (futile, empty, and meaningless) and death as an erasure of all profit from a lifetime of toil. These books are the product of centuries, with much of Proverbs being preserved orally at first, perhaps also Job 1–2.[4] Readers who are familiar with the Apocrypha, mostly Roman Catholic and Orthodox, will add Sirach (Ecclesiasticus) and Wisdom of Solomon.[5] These two books were composed in the second and first centuries BCE, an era when Hellenistic philosophy and Judaism competed for the minds of the curious in a complex society. The two

[4] The pre-literary stage of biblical wisdom has been studied by Claus Westermann, *Roots of Wisdom: The Oldest Proverbs of Israel and Other Peoples* (Louisville, KY: Westminster John Knox, 1990) and Timothy J. Sandoval, "The Orality of Wisdom Literature," 267–285 in Samuel L. Adams and Matthew Goff, eds. *The Wiley Blackwell Companion to Wisdom Literature* (Hoboken, NJ: Wiley Blackwell, 2020).

[5] Nearly two-thirds of Sirach in Hebrew has survived, including fragments discovered at Qumran and Masada. The Greek text of Wisdom of Solomon is preserved in the great majuscule manuscripts Vaticanus, Sinaiticus, and Alexandrinus.

centuries were rife with political jockeying for power and the inevitable unrest among the weak.

Because the Hebrew Bible originated in a culture deeply influenced by the neighbors with whom the Israelites interacted daily, sometimes willingly and often under duress, modern interpreters have mined the surviving literature from ancient Egypt and Mesopotamia for views like those in biblical wisdom. They naturally attached the label "wisdom Literature" to the texts that used the word wisdom while offering advice to the young or wrestling with existential issues like life's meaning and the justice of God (theodicy). Although specialists of texts from the ancient Near East consider the label somewhat misleading because in these non-biblical texts magic and cultic manipulation of the gods play an important role, they do not deny their fundamental kinship in language and attitude with biblical wisdom.[6] Can belief in only one God fit into the intellectual world of sages? After all, they seem to have made peace with polytheism for more than three millennia at least in Egypt and Mesopotamia. Biblical wisdom began at a time when henotheism, the belief in one God but not denying that other gods existed, reigned. Wisdom flourished as monotheism made an appearance in the late sixth century BCE, possibly to protest polytheism in Babylonian exile. One could even call monotheism and outlier.

One of the ironies of history is that wisdom literature emerged in a polytheistic environment. Belief in many gods divides people; wisdom unites them, preventing chaos. The two worldviews clashed from the very beginning. With mythic tales describing the exploits of divine heroes circulating everywhere, wise teachers in the civilizations nourished by three great rivers (Tigris, Euphrates, and Nile) focused a spotlight on the human potential to shape character. That this light was not extinguished for over three millennia attests to the high value placed on character formation and wrestling with existential questions.[7]

The desire to be wise lies deep within, but gaining wisdom requires individual choice and discipline. The earliest path to broader knowledge was by observing how things work and compiling lists of analogies from nature, animals, and personal relationships. As information accumulated over many lifetimes, witty individuals coined insights into parallel couplets. Poets turned oral sayings into literature, using similes to illustrate kinship among different

---

6 Wilfred G. Lambert, *Babylonian Wisdom Literature* (Oxford: Clarendon Press, 1960), 1 ("Wisdom is strictly a misnomer as applied to Mesopotamian literature. Generally, 'wisdom' refers to skill in cult and magic lore, and the wise man is the initiate"). Giorgio Buccellati, "Wisdom and Not: The Case of Mesopotamia," *Journal of the American Oriental Society* 101 (1981), 35–47 prefers the word "attitude" to describe the relationship.

7 See William P. Brown, *Character in Crisis: A Fresh Approach to the Wisdom Literature of the Old Testament* (Grand Rapids, MI: Eerdmans, 1996).

things, rhetorical questions to engage listeners, and brief narration to sustain attention. Gathered over time, the collections helped parents and teachers change lives for the common good. Leaders adopted the mix of instruction and aphorisms to achieve success in reaching reluctant students. While this was happening, a parallel phenomenon was taking place. Case law grew into an authoritative body of knowledge aiding judicial decisions. By the second century BCE, law and wisdom were brought together as one.[8] Provisional authority of parents and teachers, grounded in experience, now became absolute, teachings viewed as divinely ordained. This new stance conflicted with learning from experience alone.

A purely objective approach to existence misses hidden truth that transcends sight and sound, the two avenues to knowledge. Sages quickly added another path to understanding that involves the emotions of interpersonal relationships, the ups and downs of daily life. At the same time, they were fully aware of the dangers posed by extreme passion. To be truly wise, one must navigate verbalized inner responses to success and loss, health and sickness, friendship and alienation, and confirmation of comforting belief and its collapse. Together, the two approaches, objective and subjective, helped receptive individuals become a little wiser.

One can say that wonder is the heartbeat of wisdom, awe, and amazement over the mystery of the universe about which even God in the book of Job could not remain silent.[9] Majestic creatures with mysterious names like Behemoth and Leviathan fill the sea and marshes, fearless stallions eagerly await combat, agile mountain goats roam freely, and birds soar high above them all. The attraction of the human body, the beauty of an infant's smile, the endurance of parental love enabling a child to experience life's excitement – these wonders and more defy description. So does healing that takes place when family and friends gather around the table for a meal. Belief in divine creation lies at the center of wisdom, as do the wonders of the good earth. These things needed to be conveyed to the young.

Because biblical wisdom was deeply influenced by similar texts from Mesopotamia and Egypt, where polytheism reigned, a brief survey of these ancient texts and their impact on Israel's sages may partially explain why sages found it difficult to adjust to the introduction of revelation into rational discourse.

---

[8] James L. Crenshaw, "Law in the Wisdom Tradition," 289–307 in Pamela Barmash, ed. *The Oxford Handbook of Biblical Law* (Oxford: University Press, 2019).

[9] William P. Brown, *Wisdom's Wonder: Character, Creation, and Crisis in the Bible's Wisdom Literature* (Grand Rapids, MI: Eerdmans, 2014).

The earliest instructions, Suruppak (attributed to Ziusudra, the Sumerian hero of the flood), and Kagemni, said to be the work of a Pharaoh Ptahhotep (twenty-fifth century BCE) consist of advice and motivation. The maxims about basic virtues, expressed in a realistic tone, are expected to be passed on to the next generation. The addressee, "my son," occurs often, lending the teachings paternal authority.[10] The authority of these texts, however, rested on their ability to pass the test of time, bringing success as promised. Professional scribes took on an aura of authority, threatening lazy or disinterested students with harsh physical punishment. A sage named Ahiqar, mentioned in the Book of Tobit, whose sayings are partially preserved in Aramaic, compares whippings to manure in a garden.[11]

Sages did not hesitate to discuss the frailties of the body. Ironically, Ptahhotep's first words from the cradle of the second major genre in Egypt, behind Autobiography, as it were, complain about the unpleasantness of old age.

> O King, my Lord! Age is here, old age arrived,
> Feebleness came, weakness grows, childlike one sleeps all day. Eyes are dim, ears deaf. Strength is waning through weariness. The mouth, silenced, speaks not. The heart, void, recalls not the past. The bones ache throughout. Good has become evil, all taste is gone. What age does to people is evil in everything. The nose, clogged, breathes not; painful are standing and sitting.[12]

The authoritative voice, either that of a ruler or a parent, drowns out that of those to whom teachings were addressed, with only two known exceptions. The son in the Akkadian *Instruction of Shurpe Ameli* responds irreverently, and Khonshotep, Anii's son, says his father sets before him a difficult path, an ideal that may be beyond reach. It appears that the objection was introduced to be refuted. Anii tells Khonshotep that wild beasts can be domesticated and people who speak a different language can learn Egyptian. Even crooked sticks can be straightened, he adds. It seems that Anii understood what *Papyrus Insinger* put into words: "No instruction can succeed if there is dislike" (8:24).[13]

Where instruction took place is unclear. Some scholars use meager evidence of early writing to suggest that widespread schools existed in Israel despite the absence of any reference to schools until the second century. Even this remark by Ben Sira has been understood as an allusion to the book he left for posterity

---

[10] Miriam Lichtheim, *Ancient Egyptian Literature*, Vol. 1 (Berkeley, CA: University of California Press, 1975), 63–80.

[11] See Seth A. Bledsoe, "Ahiqar and Other Legendary Sages," 289–309 in Samuel L. Adams and Matthew Goff, eds. *The Wiley Blackwell Companion to Wisdom Literature* (London: Wiley Blackwell, 2020) and James M. Lindenberger, *The Aramaic Proverbs of Ahiqar* (Baltimore, MD: Johns Hopkins University, 1998).

[12] Lichtheim, *Ancient Egyptian Literature*, 3, 192. [13] 13 Ibid., Vol. 1, 62–63.

("Draw near to me, you who are untaught, and lodge in my school," Sir 51:23). It is likely that a few scribes were able to train enough young boys for royal administration during the short time before the fall of Jerusalem. Formal education for all was long in coming.[14]

Instructions and maxims were based on experience, but life always brings exceptions to every supposed rational rule. Undesirable consequences are also the result of experience, which teaches us that such a rule for coping with eventualities can never be found with absolute certainty. One must always be open to new experiences. Because the stakes are so high, enthusiasts run the risk of dogmatic rigidity. Sages were not oblivious to this danger.

There is evidence of the sages' perspective concerning the deity in these texts. For example, realists among the sages questioned the optimism behind instructions and even divine justice, leading to vanity literature, the consequence of intellectual freedom among literati. *The Babylonian Theodicy* (eleventh century BCE) consists of twenty-seven stanzas of eleven lines each. It pursues the question that haunts the biblical Job and concludes that one cannot know the will of the gods.

> The mind of the god, like the center of the heavens, is remote;
> Knowledge of it is very difficult; people cannot know it . . . .
> Narru . . . and majestic Zulummar . . . and goddess Mami . . .
> Gave twisted speech to the human race.
> With lies, and not truth, they endowed them forever.[15]

The same theme is taken up in *Ludlul,* also known as *I Will Praise the Lord of Wisdom*.

> I wish I knew that these things would be pleasing to one's god!
> What is good for oneself may be offense to one's god.
> What in one's own heart seems despicable may be proper to one's god.
> Who can know the will of the gods in heaven?
> Who can understand the plans of the underworld gods?
> Where have humans learned the way of a god?[16]

The consequence of this epistemology is dire, for it undercuts the sages' pedagogy. The irony of praising the Lord of Wisdom while acknowledging that humans are clueless about the will of the gods is poignant. Will reason's restraint lead to humility? This awareness of the limits to reasons' capabilities

[14] See James L. Crenshaw, *Education in Ancient Israel: Across the Deadening Silence*. ABRL (New York: Doubleday, 1998). For schools, see 85–113, pedagogy, 115–138, resistance to learning, 139–185, the language for intellectual achievement, 205–219.

[15] Norman B. Pritchard, ed. *Ancient Near Eastern Texts Relating to the Old Testament*. 3rd ed. (Princeton, NJ: Princeton University, 1969), 267.

[16] Ibid., 266.

will lead to a partial resolution in the time of Ben Sira and Pseudo-Solomon. Drawing on Greek philosophy, they will appeal to cosmic order, yoking it with divine decree, or law, to be discussed later.

The Sumerian *Nothing of Value* recommends two options: carpe diem or become more religious. The latter anticipates Pascal's famous wager which is based on covering all the bases just in case there is a God. *The Pessimistic Dialogue* pushes vanity literature to the extreme: considering suicide. In this text, a master and a slave discuss contrasting possibilities, and the slave dismisses whatever the master proposes, suggesting the opposite. Scholars differ about its genre, whether parody or humor, for it ends with the master proposing to kill the servant first. His response: "Then (I swear) my master will not outlive me by even three days."[17]

Late Egyptian Demotic texts, *Papyrus Insinger* and *The Sayings of Ankhsheshonq* (634–332 BCE) introduce fate as the determiner of destiny. Success was no longer believed to be guaranteed by living right. From *Papyrus Insinger* we read "The fate and fortune that comes, it is the god that sends them."[18] Like *Ptahhotep, Papyrus Insinger* comments on old age ("He who has passed sixty years, everything has passed for him").[19] It divides the first forty years of life into decades: the first, childhood, the second, school, the third, work, the fourth, maturing, the next sixty, a gift of Thoth, God of wisdom. These texts demonstrate that the wise were not just interested in individual success. They tried to bring together in some meaningful way cause and effect, the natural and supernatural. A stable society mattered to them ("He who raves with the crowd is not called a fool" {*Papyrus Insinger* 4:11}; "Do not disdain a small document, a small fire, a small soldier" *Ankhsheshonq* {16:25}). The paradoxical formulations in *Insinger* and *Ankhsheshonq* fuse morality and piety.

Wisdom literature is distinct in that it fails to view history as the end all and be all of existence. This indifference to history does not secure the texts from the effects of history. In fact, a development of views on God/gods is evidenced with the passing of time as reflected in many ancient texts. For example, with the passing of time, the pharaohs and viziers credited with instructions introduced new themes related to their perspectives of the deity (or deities) and their changing social and cultural settings. *The Testament of Amenemhet* (2040–1650) commiserates to his son Sesotris about a palace coup that took place in the thirtieth year of his reign. In *Merikare*, a royal testament that is pseudepigraphic, Cheti tells his son about a judgment after death. Most importantly, the ethical principle of justice and retribution becomes increasingly dominant. In Mesopotamia, the Sumerian collection of instructions broadened the net to

[17] Ibid., 601. [18] Lichtheim, *Ancient Egyptian Literature,* Vol. 3, 191. [19] Ibid., 199.

include riddles, jokes, folktales, fables, and humor. One example reveals the teachers' wit: What does one enter with closed eyes and depart with open eyes? A school. Egyptian sages were also capable of humor. *The Satire of the Trades* refers to the work of a potter as grubbing in the mud more than pigs, the lot of a weaver worse than a woman, and that of a farmer as wailing more than a guinea fowl.

These evolving themes reveal at least one thing concerning the connection between the sages' understanding of the divine and the wisdom literature they produced. They reflect ancient sages' effort to yoke together a realistic view of daily experience and some acknowledgment that a supreme authority validated the insights acquired by reason alone. They raise the question attributed to a famous rabbi, Hillel: "Am I for myself alone, or is someone else for me?"

A glance at these ancient texts reveals a striking absence: a speaking deity, with one exception. The biblical Job wrangles a response from God, albeit out of a whirlwind. The Babylonian and Sumerian parallels to Job do not contain a speaking god. Wisdom literature is primarily the voice of reason, not revelation. It is the closest thing to modern science with knowledge based on experience. No individual is excluded from its domain, for every human is endowed with a brain and is subject to the rules of physics, chemistry, and biology. The Egyptian God ma'at was believed to have established a cosmic order that rewards good behavior and punishes bad conduct. Everyone, that is, bears responsibility for her or his own success or failure.

Did the authors of wisdom literature in the Bible know any of these texts from Egypt and Mesopotamia? The answer is an emphatic "yes" in at least one case, the Egyptian *Instruction of Amenemope* and Proverbs. The brief collection of sayings in Prov 22:17–24:22 contains ten indisputable borrowings plus a similar introduction that probably refers to thirty, the number of chapters in *Amenemope*. In addition to warning against removing landmarks and associating with hot-tempered men, the sayings refer to riches that take wings and fly to heaven, a blocking (hair) to the throat, and they promise that a skilled scribe will serve royalty.

What about the authors of Job and Ecclesiastes? *The Babylonian Theodicy* and Job are both structurally and substantively similar. In each, a dialogue between a sufferer and a friend takes place, although the number of friends differs (four in Job, two in *The Babylonian Theodicy*). The problem, however, is the same one that has troubled humanity for millennia, the suffering of the innocent. Where injustice exists, it seems that either God (or the gods) does not care or cannot do anything about it. That circumstance leads to charges that the Shepherd has abandoned the sheep in *The Protests of the Eloquent Peasant* and to questions about both human nature and the divine. Assumptions about the individual's capacity to understand the way the world works and convictions about power and goodness suddenly become suspect. Facing up to oppressive reality may lead to renewed devotion, as in *Ludlul*, or to defiance, which seems to be Job's response. When literary problems are involved, literary dependence is difficult to prove, although nearly direct identity such as that found in Job's negative confession in chapter 31 and that in the Egyptian Book of the Dead, chapter 125 ("I have not robbed, coveted, stolen, killed people, trimmed the measure, cheated, lied, committed adultery") lends credibility to at least minimal influence.

As for Ecclesiastes, a few similarities may lead to raised eyebrows but fall short of definitive proof of dependence. By modern standards, *Ptahhotep's* lame description of old age pales in comparison to Qoheleth's poetry in 12:1–8 describing old age and dying, but a Sumerian text resembles the biblical one in at least one line of symbolic poetry.

> (I was) a youth (but now) . . . my black mountain has produced white gypsum . . .
> My teeth which used to chew strong things can no more chew strong things.

*The Dispute of a Man with his Soul* resembles Qoheleth's interior monologue, as does the emphasis on death. From Emar, *Enlil and Namzitarra* urges people to seize the day because of fixed and immutable human destinies. The Egyptian *Complaints of Khakherperre Sonbe* refers to gathering words and expresses a desire for new vocabulary to replace what has been said.

> The gathering of words . . . Had I unknown phrases, sayings that are strange,
> novel, untried words that are free of repetition . . . for what was said is repetition.[20]

The meaning of the Hebrew word Qoheleth, a noun based on the verbal root meaning "to gather," and his observation that there is nothing new under the sun link the texts. Above all, there is the advice to cast bread on the waters, together with the promise of getting it back, in both Qoheleth and *Ankhsheshonq*. That life is a puff of wind, recognized by Qoheleth and a Mesopotamian sage, is a natural conclusion to anyone who reflects on the connection between breathing and being alive. The observation that a threefold cord is not easily broken, known from Mesopotamia and Qoheleth, may also be common knowledge.

What about Sirach, the only author of biblical wisdom whose name and historical circumstances are known? The prologue to the book, written by Ben Sira's grandson, enables us to date the book around 185 BCE, about fifteen years before the Maccabean revolt against the Syrian leader Antiochus Epiphanes. Within a decade and half, the Hasmonean dynasty was established,

[20] Ibid., 146.

and Jewish home rule lasted until the Romans seized power in the first century BCE. Ben Sira was familiar with the Egyptian *Satire of the Trades*, which reveals the extent to which intellectual snobbery existed in ancient times. The scribe contrasts his exalted position with that of laborers in carpentry, crafts, smiths, pottery, architecture, the military, and so forth. In Sir 38:24–34, Ben Sira exhibits more respect for workers than does the Egyptian counterpart. In his words, “they keep stable the fabric of the world.”

Other similarities with Egyptian texts occur in Sirach such as the advice not to make friends with a merchant since his purpose in life is to take a slice from merchandise or to charge for a drink of water, an attitude stretching back to the ancient Sumerians (*Ankhsheshonq* 28:4, 16:5 and Sir 26:29; 27:2). To defend God’s justice, Ben Sira employs a debate tactic common in Egypt, the expression “Do not say,” followed by something aimed at easing theodicy (*Ankhsheshonq* 3:16, “Do not say, ‘The sinner against God lives today, but look to the end’”).

Living in Alexandria, the author of Wisdom of Solomon, called Pseudo Solomon by some interpreters, was completely at home in a Hellenistic environment. Writing in Greek, he takes for granted the four cardinal virtues of self-control, prudence, justice, and courage. He presupposes the ordering principle of the universe, *logos* (word) to Stoics but names it/her *Sophia* (wisdom). From Middle Platonism he takes over the concept of an intermediary entity related to both realms, heaven and earth. He also accepts the idea of an immortal soul weighed down by the body, and he believes in a postmortem judgment.

This kinship between biblical wisdom and texts from the other cultures in the ancient Near East should surprise no one, given the readiness to compare Solomon, the biblical sage par excellence in popular thought, to other near-Eastern sages. His alleged superiority in what can be called “nature wisdom” is proclaimed in 1Kgs 5:9–14. He is said to be wiser than all the Kedemites, Egyptians, and four individuals he names who are said to be renowned for wisdom but from whom no texts have survived. Solomon is credited with composing 3,000 proverbs and 1,005 songs. Their content, trees, birds, beasts, creeping things, and fish, bears little resemblance to sayings attributed to Solomon in Proverbs and even less in Ecclesiastes and Wisdom of Solomon. Considering the ancient tendency to credit rulers with literary achievements, many modern interpreters doubt the reliability of the observations about Solomon’s literary expertise.

Even Proverbs includes two brief collections said to be of foreign venue (30:1–14; 31:1–9) and another (22:17–24:22) with the heading “the sayings of the wise” but which derive in part from *Amenemope.* The other two identify the authors as Agur son of Jakeh from Massa and an unnamed mother of Lemuel, king of Massa. Agur also professes a lack of ordinary intelligence and knowledge of the deity. He alludes to a myth about a heavenly figure descending to earth, familiar from biblical prophecy and Wisdom of Solomon. He also wonders who has control of wind and water, often thought to be the domain of Baal. Lemuel's mother warns her son against wasting energy on women and strong drinks. In her view, he should save his strength for aiding the poor and attending to judicial responsibility, a common expectation of royalty in the ancient world.

The other collections in Proverbs are ascribed to Solomon (1:1–9:18; 10:1–22:16; 25:1–29:27) and to unnamed wise men (24:23–34), or they lack a superscription (30:15–33; 31:10–31). The third collection in Solomon's name gives the additional information that men of Hezekiah transcribed them. Such scribal activity at the royal court is likely, for kings needed knowledgeable people to carry out normal administrative duties, especially keeping accurate tax records, and to supervise propaganda.

Foreign wisdom is on display in the book of Job. The hero is from the land of Uz, presumably in Edom, renowned for wisdom, but no sapiential texts have survived from there. The three friends who come to console him are from foreign countries. Eliphaz is a Temanite, Bildad a Shuhite, and Zophar a Naamathite. Moreover, the author of the poetic debate studiously avoids the special name YHWH, using it only when the Judean, Elihu, and God speak.

Although the author of Ecclesiastes chooses Solomon as his persona, he quickly drops this identity and speaks like an ordinary citizen subject to a king. The language confirms the suspicion that Solomon had nothing to do with the book. Its closest linguistic parallel is from rabbinic texts, leading one scholar to write that if Solomon wrote Ecclesiastes the history of the Hebrew language cannot be written. The book was probably written during the first half of the third century BCE, possibly a century earlier.

A few scholars have broadened the body of wisdom literature to include Song of Songs, Deuteronomy, the Joseph story, segments of Amos and Isaiah, and even Esther. Others have denied its existence as a genre altogether.[21] It remains to be seen whether this assault on the existence of the genre will gain momentum. At the very least, Proverbs, Job, and Ecclesiastes differ from the rest of the canon, saying nothing about a covenant between YHWH and Israel, patriarchs Abraham and Isaac, divine commandments conveyed through Moses, or the

[21] Will Kynes, *An Obituary for Wisdom Literature: The Birth, Death, and Intertextual Reintegration of a Biblical Corpus* (Oxford University Press, 2019) and Stuart Weeks, "Is 'Wisdom Literature a useful Category?'", 3–23 in Hindy Najman, Jean-Sebastian Rey, and Eibert J. C. Tigehelaar, eds. *Tracing Sapiential Traditions in Ancient Judaism,* JSJ Sups 174 (Leiden: Brill, 2016).

Davidic monarchy. Nor do they view history as guided by God to benefit a chosen people, directly or through prophetic messengers.

The conservative Ben Sira breaks with earlier sages and incorporates Jewish history into his teachings. His praise of heroes in 44–50 gives pride of place to priests like Aaron and Phineas. Following the sequence of the three divisions in the Hebrew Bible, he mentions individuals who appear in the Pentateuch (where one finds the ordering of the material universe into the cosmos by gods or God, the formation of humans, the myths and legends of ancestors, and the law and cult), Prophets (the establishing of the state, its officials and spiritual leadership, the union under three kings, and its rupture, the separate history of Israel and Judah, and their fall to Assyria and Babylon), before moving on to the third division, Writings (the laments, three wisdom books, apocalyptic texts, a novella, erotic songs, and revised imaginary history). The sage's admiration for the High Priest Simon moves him to elevate Aaron over Moses, although he makes room for the Torah, equating it with wisdom. His highest praise goes to personified Wisdom, whose grandeur he extols in five hymns. Once he has linked wisdom with an identifiable people, the Jews, and a special deity, he goes a step further. He prays that favor be shown to Abraham's descendants at their enemies' expense, strange for a sage.

While Ben Sira takes pains to identify the heroes in the hymn and others mentioned elsewhere in his teachings, Pseudo-Solomon credits his readers with sufficient knowledge to recognize the individuals to whom he refers. In a section on divine providence (11:6–19:21), he contrasts God's favorable treatment of the Jews with the harsh treatment of Egyptians. Like Ben Sira, he believed that God turned toward Jews with a merciful countenance. For this author, who lives in an age of flourishing idol worship, the failure to recognize the true God brings horrible consequences.

The collective memory of a nation reaches into the distant past, especially concerning things like beginnings and threatened endings. Those who chose to record sacred memories in ancient Israel preserved bits and pieces of myths that can be traced back to Egyptian, Canaanite, Assyrian, Babylonian, and Sumerian literature. The combination of contact through diplomatic relations and daily encounters with merchants from foreign lands kept these memories alive. With the deciphering of hieroglyphics, cuneiform, and Ugaritic script, the many similarities between biblical stories and ancient Near Eastern literature became known to scholars.

The little touches, like the snake devouring a branch from the tree of life that Gilgamesh set aside long enough to take a swim in a local pool correspond to the clever snake's role in preventing Adam and Eve from becoming immortal. The advice by Ea, God of wisdom, in the Babylonian story of the flood that led

Utnapishtim to build a boat is replicated in YHWH's counsel to Noah. The creation of mortals from clay and divine blood in *Enuma Elish* is like YHWH's forming the first human from clay. The creation of heaven and earth from Tiamat's body is like Elohim's use of preexistent material, called *tohu* and *bohu,* to bring order out of chaos.

The self-praise by Isis prefigures Wisdom's boasts in Proverbs, just as ma'at's place and function in the Egyptian pantheon is like that of personified Wisdom. The landing place of the boat after the flood subsided (Mt. Ararat) and the sending of birds to test the decline of the waters are the same in extrabiblical and biblical stories. The council of gods in Ugaritic texts, Mesopotamian sources, and the Bible functions in an identical manner. The decline of longevity among postdiluvian populations in the Sumerian texts and the Bible differs only in number of years. The sexual relations between gods and humans and the building of towers to heaven (ziggurats) link the Bible to Mesopotamia. The interchangeable names and epithets for gods like El, Shamash, and Baal indicate politico-morphism, the result of close contact. Such correspondence proves that cultural intermixing was not restricted to one genre, wisdom or otherwise.

No evidence exists for monotheism in Mesopotamia, and only one dubious example in Egypt has survived in the extensive literature dating from the fourth to the second millennium. However, tension between polytheism and unification of deities and their attributes existed in Egypt. Syncretistic worship eased the tension to some degree. With urbanization in Mesopotamia, a similar unification occurred. With Pharaoh Amenophis IV (1350–1334) that tension reached a breaking point. He changed his name to Akhenaten, moved the capital to Amarna, and ordered that the names of all other gods be erased from public view. He sought to elevate the worship of the solar disk (Re) at the exclusion of all other gods. In practice, however, only he and his wife could worship Re. Other Egyptians were expected to worship him and perhaps the sun god indirectly. His radical departure from precedent was so unpopular that at his death Egyptians returned to the adoration of multiple deities.

Although polytheism was practiced in the ancient Near East, it always had a component that opened the door to monotheism by way of henotheism. Once the worship of elements in nature (sun, moon, wind, and so forth) declined as empires emerged, the God of the strongest ruler was believed to be the High God, and other gods served in his council. A beautiful expression of adoration occurs in the *Hymn to the Aten* ("Though you are far, your rays are on earth, though one sees you, your strides are unseen . . . O Sole God beside whom there is none . . . How excellent are your ways, O Lord of eternity").[22] The existence of other gods does not really matter to this worshipper. That is precisely the situation in the Hebrew Bible where the divine council is implied (Gen 1,1 Kgs 22, the prologue to Job, and Isaiah 40–55). The path to High God was paved with acts of violence, with the victor taking over the name and powers of the defeated. In this way YHWH replaced the Canaanite deity Baal, just as Marduk and other gods assumed the powers of rivals. The Bible has preserved a host of these names while showing preference for YHWH in Judah and Elohim in Ephraim.

The period from 800 to 200 BCE has been called the Axial Age, a time when the dominance of kings and priests, palaces and temples, waned. In their place a merchant class rose to prominence, with the exchange of goods, both practical and exotic, being brought from afar by traveling merchants. In the Indian subcontinent, the Vedic gods were being superseded by religious teachers as the Vedanta came into existence by the fifth century. About 538 BCE Siddhartha Gautama became a mendicant ascetic, soon gaining enlightenment and urging his disciples to save themselves by learning to control their inner selves. In Greece Plato (ca. 428–348 BCE) was busy defending Socrates and teaching about forms approximating an Absolute, ideals such as Beauty and the Good. Three-quarters of a century later Aristotle emphasized the catharsis of emotions like terror and pity, in a sense achieving a new birth. In Israel and Judah, the Axial Age saw the rise of prophetic calls for social justice, compassion, and the individual conscience. Views of deities were changing as aggressive economies competed with one another, and human life was thought to contain an essential transcendent element.[23]

Was monotheism also vulnerable to alternative views? Two things suggest an affirmative answer. First, the presence of evil in excess threw into question God's goodness and power, as the third-century Greek philosopher Epicurus recognized long before Voltaire mocked Leibniz in *Candide*. What was needed to exonerate the High God for such wickedness? Someone else to blame. The Persian king Cyrus did more than free Judean exiles by defeating Babylon in 539 BCE, for the religious views of the people he ruled introduced Judeans to the concept of dualism, the answer being sought by monotheists to explain the presence of so much pain and suffering in a supposed perfect world. The key was to make one significant rival subject to the Sovereign Deity. An antagonist emerged from a nameless rebel in Job who would become known as Satan in

[22] William W. Hallo, ed. *The Context of Scripture: Canonical Compositions from the Biblical World,* Vol. 1 (Leiden: Brill, 2003), 44–46.

[23] Karen Armstrong, *A History of God: The 4,000-Year Quest of Judaism, Christianity, and Islam* (New York: Ballantine Books, 1993), 27.

Zechariah and Chronicles. Second, the prominence in wisdom literature of an intermediary figure, *Hokmah/Sophia/Logos* blurred the distinction between God and her. This emanation of God in female form represents an attempt to bring together reason and revelation.

## 1 Dualism and a Divine Female Persona

### 1.1 Dualism

Individuals in the ancient world were bombarded with contrasts: heaven/earth, male/female, good/bad, near/far, light/darkness, and so on. The priestly account of creation in Gen 1:1–2:4a refers to a primordial duality which it calls "waste and void" and from which God fashioned an orderly universe. Confronted with multiple dualities, people must have considered the possibility that dualism existed in divinity too. Myths of creation in Egypt and Mesopotamia use images of birthing that necessarily imply gender among Gods.

Stories about the origin of the universe from Israel and her neighbors usually involve sex or conflict between rivals. One Egyptian version refers to onanism by which Atum supplies seed to Mother Earth; a rival version has Ptah issue a commanding word. The former view was at home in Heliopolis, the other in Memphis. The Mesopotamian *Enuma Elish* describes a struggle between the gods Apsu and Tiamat, who represent fresh water and salt water. The victor splits Tiamat apart, forming the two dimensions of the cosmos from her body. As an afterthought, Marduk creates humans from the blood of the rather stupid god, Kingu, Tiamat's consort. What caused the conflict? The young gods were too noisy, interrupting their parents' sleep. Although presented as a kind of population control, the myth reflects an annual event, the flooding of the Tigris and Euphrates in the spring.

Population control also lies behind the myth in Genesis but is given a moral twist like the story of the tower of Babel. Divine beings and humans intermarry, producing giants and angering God, who sends a flood that destroys everyone but Noah and his family. Survivors are said to have their life expectancy lowered to 120 years. This contrasts with a much greater reduction in Sumerian lore. God may decry the crossing of boundaries and the resulting evil inclination, but his extreme reaction exposes a dark side.

Stories that imply ambivalence in the biblical God appear too frequently to ignore. Over time, they posed an ethical dilemma with huge theological implications, at least to men like Philo, the unknown author of Second Esdras, and the early rabbis living in a Hellenized environment. For them, a question arose: Can the deity's conduct be justified? The people who heard such stories must have thought God did not command Abraham to sacrifice his son, Isaac, seek to kill

Moses, send a lying spirit to the prophet opposing Micaiah ben Imlah, harass Saul with an evil spirit, display partiality to Abel, destroy the cities of Sodom and Gomorrah without removing the innocent, and so on.

Such descriptions of disturbing conduct on God's part were borne out in words attributed to God, who claims to have created both weal and woe.[24] Although intended to prove the uniqueness of God, they lead to quite different thoughts. Even the two epithets "warrior" and "healer" in the story about YHWH's victory over Pharaoh and his subjects (Exod 15:3,26) reflect ambivalence, for innocent children among the victims died too. The sages must have asked: Should divine favor not be universal? A later rabbi certainly saw the impropriety of Miriam's song praising YHWH when his own children were dying in the sea.

A second factor compounding the impression made by divine ambivalence is YHWH's claim to incomparability (Exod 15:11). According to it, nothing on earth or in heaven is equal to him. If true, it means that evil must be traced to the only God who exists. The heavy hand of YHWH may fall on enemies of Israel (Exod 15:12), but they are his children too. The extension of YHWH's power over all other gods in Ps 95:3 reinforces the idea that no one is comparable to this Sovereign. In such a scenario, the presence of other deities requires a response. The easiest reaction is to do nothing. Toleration, polytheism's generous attitude to other gods, demands no effort and results in the status quo.

To some degree, these troublesome features help explain the durability of polytheism even when apologists for a high God let their voice be heard and emperors made exclusive adoration mandatory for those seeking favor. Iconoclasts in remote areas of civilization would have continued to worship local minor deities. Evidence of devotion to YHWH and a female deity Asherah has survived at two outposts, Quntillet Azrud and Khirbet-'el Qom and on the island of Elephantine in the Nile delta. The prophet Ezekiel mentions a bolder act of what he considered apostasy, one taking place in the holy city and sacred temple. Even priests of the official religion retained vestiges of an earlier deity, Baal.

Reluctance to abandon some aspects of Canaanite religion was behind the story about the fashioning of an idol, a golden bull, in Moses's absence. The same attempt to retain a revered tradition takes the form of verbal expressions; two of Baal's specialties attributed to YHWH are noteworthy. He treads on the

[24] Eric A Seibert, *Disturbing Divine Behavior: Troubling Old Testament Images of God* (Minneapolis, MN: Fortress Press, 2007) and Michael Bergmann, Michael J. Murray, and Michael C. Ray, eds. *Divine Evil? The Moral Character of the God of Abraham* (Oxford: Oxford University Press, 2011) indicate the impossibility of finding satisfactory answers to the dark side of God in the Bible.

back of the god Yamm, also the name of the sea, and makes the wind his chariot. In Psalm 29 YHWH has completely taken over Baal's attributes and sits enthroned over the floodwaters, having defeated Baal. His victory is memorialized in Elijah's contest with the 450 prophets of Baal. Similarly, Psalm 104 views YHWH as having embodied the awesome attributes of the Egyptian sun God celebrated in the beautiful hymn to the sun.

Long before monotheism began to appear in Judah, incipient monotheism existed. The eighth-century prophet Amos thinks YHWH has sovereignty over other nations (Amos 9:7). His near contemporary Isaiah believes that YHWH uses Assyria to punish disobedient Israelites but destroys the mighty Assyrian army when Sennacherib goes too far, a legend that Byron immortalized for readers of a much later era. It was left to the author of Daniel to assert YHWH's sovereignty over the gods of Babylon. With Deutero-Isaiah, the poet who experiences the optimism of a formerly subject people tasting freedom once more, thanks to the Persian king Cyrus, YHWH emerges as the high God, but with that exaltation also come the troubling attributes. About two centuries before the Hebrew canon was closed the author of Chronicles seems to have felt a need to remove what to him was egregious. He rewrites the account in second Samuel 24:1 where YHWH incites David to take a census of the citizens in Jerusalem and then punishes him for doing so. In the Chronicler's telling, Satan persuades David to take the census in First Chronicles 21:1 to explain away conduct attributed elsewhere to Greek gods that was no longer considered acceptable to Judeans. The first-century Jewish Philosopher, Philo, achieves the same result by resorting to allegory.

Enthusiasm over YHWH's exclusiveness must have been tempered by revered texts such as Elohim's remark "Let us make humankind in our likeness" and "male and female he made them." The divine council is taken for granted in the priestly creation story. In addition, the proliferation of angels in the Pseudepigrapha opened the door for a rebel to challenge God. Both Isaiah and Ezekiel refer to this heavenly rogue and his fall to earth, a myth that is explored at great lengths by John Milton in *Paradise Lost*. Isaiah 14 uses a Canaanite myth about the day star and dawn to mock the aspirations of an unnamed egoist who aspired to divinity but fell to ignominy in Sheol. The ascent to heaven's mount of assembly in the mysterious north and the adoption of the name Most High like Baal the Lord of heaven are followed by a descent to the pit. Similarly, Ezekiel 28 depicts the Prince of Tyre as one endowed with divine entitlements, wiser than Danel, a legendary hero in Ugaritic texts, and occupying a seat on the mountain of God. Because pride replaced wisdom in the mind of this figure, 'adonai YHWH cast him out of heaven to the earth below.

While the clever serpent in Genesis 3 is said to have persuaded Eve to disobey her creator and partake of the forbidden fruit, the curse condemns it to permanent animosity toward humans that takes the form of a snake bite. It was left to the rabbis to contemplate the serpent as humaniform and thus able to implant an evil seed in Eve. A concept of original sin came to characterize Christian theologians, with ruinous consequences, especially for women.

A rebellious figure called Satan in Hebrew provides an antagonist capable of persuasion like the serpent but also powerful enough to wreak havoc when given a measure of freedom by God as in Job 1–2. The word Satan carries the connotation of slander in Job 1–2, Numbers 22: 22, 32, but Zechariah 3:1–2 has a lamer sense, accuse. In First Chronicles 21:1 incite seems preferable. Only the latter text has the article as if it is now a personal name. The other references merely refer to a slanderer or an adversary. By the time the Pseudepigraphic books of Jubilees (23:29) and Assumption of Moses (10:1) were composed in the second century BCE, Satan had become a personal name. These late texts frequently refer to demons such as Asmodeus in Tobit 3: 8, 17, Shemihazel or Azazel in 1 Enoch 6:11, and Mastema in Jubilees. Texts from Qumran prefer Belial or Beliar and picture an epic struggle between light and darkness.[25]

After a slow start under Persian influence, dualism flourished in the two centuries before the rise of Christianity and during the first couple of centuries of its formation. Unhappy with the priestly hierarchy in Jerusalem, a small group of Jews settled in the region of the Dead Sea and formed a religious community that saw itself at war with the forces of darkness and lies. Calling their leader "the teacher of righteousness," they composed a rule for communal existence heavily based on seniority of membership. They also taught the importance of meditation, with the object of their meditation being a "mystery" they expected to come. Roman soldiers threatened their existence, leading caretakers of precious documents to hide them in clay pots and bury them in several caves alongside the Dead Sea. There they lay until the late nineteen forties when a young goatherder discovered a cache of them. A thorough search of the area yielded more scrolls, most importantly a copy of the biblical book of Isaiah, as well as a book of hymns and a war manual that has been called "The Wars of the Children of Light against the Children of Darkness."[26]

[25] See Victor Hamilton, "Satan," *Anchor Bible Dictionary*, Vol. 5 (New York: Doubleday, 1992), 985–989.

[26] See Elisa Uusimaki, "Wisdom Texts from the Dead Sea Scrolls," 122–138 in The Wiley Blackwell Companion to Wisdom Literature and Matthew J. Goff, ed. *Discerning Wisdom: The Sapiential Literature of the Dead Sea Scrolls* (Leiden: Brill, 2007).

The thoroughly dualistic scroll taps into an earlier apocalyptic view of a cosmic confrontation between good and evil. Each side in this imagined conflict was to be led by someone who embodied righteousness or its opposite. In the view of the author, victory would belong to truth but not until a formidable struggle occurred. The New Testament book of Revelation imagines a similar confrontation between faithful Christians and the Antichrist, a battle to take place on the hill of Megiddo, hence the name Armageddon. The apostle Paul borrowed language from Greek philosophers about a spiritual war against vice. In his words, Christians should put on the breastplate of righteousness and fight the good fight, wrestling with the prince of this world. Even Jesus is said to have had to resist temptation from the devil who is said to be always searching for prey.

The most extensive example of dualism involved a group called Gnostics, a term derived from the Greek verb for knowledge (*gnostizo*). For these individuals, salvation came from acquiring secret knowledge. According to this philosophy, the soul was trapped in a body and had to be redeemed, not by a sacrificial act like a death on a cross but by *gnosis*. Christian Gnostics quickly multiplied in this environment. Texts from Nag Hammadi in Egypt throw light on this movement, especially *The Gospel of Thomas*, said to be a collection of Jesus' sayings.[27] In this text Jesus talks in symbolic language as in the gospel of John, unlike the Synoptic gospels. *The Hymn of the Pearl* depicts Jesus as a redeemed redeemer. He is sent to retrieve the soul, symbolized by a pearl, that is hidden in the depths of the watery abyss. On becoming incarnate, he is overcome by a drunken stupor (mortal flesh) and must be rescued by God. Only then does Jesus descend into the underworld and retrieve the soul.

In the second century CE, Marcion, an admirer of Paul, had a large following in Rome who, like their leader, believed that the creator, Yahweh, was responsible for the bad things in the world. That conclusion was inevitable if one believed that all created matter, everything material, was impure, a common belief in Hellenistic philosophy. Marcion picked and chose the texts from the New Testament that, in his view, belonged to a canon of sacred scripture. The Hebrew Bible had no place in his canon. Iranian dualism was but one problem facing monotheists. A divine female persona is also said to have originated in heaven and descended to earth, although with God's approval.

## 1.2 A Female Divine Persona

The Hebrew Bible occasionally personifies feminine nouns like righteousness and peace. Psalm 85:10 imagines them kissing, either in greeting or in

[27] Walter T. Wilson, *Ancient Wisdom* (Grand Rapids, MN: Eerdmans, 2020), 277–285.

a passionate show of affection. Cities are personified (Zion and Babel) and so are ships. The deep is called Abaddon or death and in Job 28:22 it is imagined to be a conveyor of a rumor. Sheol is pictured as a dreaded foe with an open mouth for swallowing those with whom she comes in contact.

Did a readiness to personify some things lead to a female embodiment of wisdom? Alternatively, was she the result of a desire to elevate women, one based on experience with remarkably talented wives like the one pictured in Proverbs 31:10–31? The narrative about Samson in Judges 13–16 shows that at least one other author attempted to contrast Israelite wives with rivals, in this instance foreign women. Another possibility, did Egyptian descriptions of Isis and ma'at influence the biblical author who first sang wisdom's praises as present when God created the world? Perhaps a combination of factors lies behind this intriguing figure, but the impact of ma'at can be seen in her development as the ordering principle of the universe.[28]

Like Isis whose self-pronouncements are well known, she sings her praises without apologizing for the immodesty of such extraordinary claims. According to her, she was born or fashioned as the first or best of God's works and watched the birth of the universe. While heaven and earth began to take shape, she delighted in God's presence. Perhaps she did even more than rejoice like the morning stars and all the angels in Job 38:7. The Hebrew word *'amon* in Proverbs 8:30 may suggest that she either drew the blueprint for the world or assisted in the work of creation itself. Proverbs introduces this mysterious female from two perspectives, that of an external observer and in her own words. Priority goes to what she says about herself.

The adverb *'etslo* (beside him) excludes the idea that she is an outsider as the universe emerges, even if the allusion to daily rejoicing overlooks the fact that day and night did not exist in the story of beginnings. Nor did humankind, in whom she takes delight in Proverbs 8:31. Her eyes are mostly directed at the earth (oceans, springs, mountains, dust, horizons, and the sea's boundary), even if they shift momentarily to observe the heavens and clouds.

The significance of primacy lies behind the Hebrew *'olam* in verse 23. For ancient Hebrews, authority rested in ancestors from long ago like Abraham,

[28] See Sylvia Schroer, *Wisdom Has Built Her House* (Collegeville, MN: Liturgical Press, 2000). In her view, "Personified wisdom is unthinkable without the 'wise woman' in the literature and history of Israel," 25. See also Alice M. Sinnott, *The Personification of Wisdom, Society of Old Testament Monograph Series* (Aldershot: Ashgate, 2005). She argues that the personification of Wisdom is a literary creation that serves as theodicy (173).

Enoch, and Moses. Wisdom's authority derives from eternity, just as YHWH's sovereignty is enshrined in a name, the Ancient of Days, bestowed on a son of man in Daniel 7:13. Because the teachings of the wise laid no claim to divine origin like torah and prophecy, this reinforcement of advice from a divine emissary made-up for the missing component. The external observer describes her in Proverbs 1:20–27 and 9:1–6. Wisdom stands in the marketplace and in language appropriated from prophecy addresses the young who spurn her. Those who refuse God's word will cry for help in vain during the inevitable disaster. Her words also include an invitation to a feast. Having built her house with seven pillars, prepared the food, and sent her maids to deliver invitations to prospective guests, she adds her own voice to that of her emissaries. Whom does she hope to see at her table? None other than the simple who lack understanding. The reference to seven pillars may recall wisdom's role in 8:22–31, for ancient stories about the creation are followed by the deity's construction of a temple, the universe itself and an earthly copy. In her house wisdom serves more than bread and wine, for she adds meat to the menu.

Elsewhere in Proverbs, the simple are invited to something in addition to sitting at wisdom's table. They are urged to love and embrace her in Proverbs 4: 6, 8 and 7:4 like a sister, to which one may compare Song of Songs' use of sister as lover. Naturally, this metaphoric language was subject to yet another use, that of seduction. Proverbs 9:13–18 reveals the extent to which it backfired, producing a rival to wisdom. Folly, too, is personified. She is adept at persuasive speech, especially its suggestive metaphor. Having chosen a vantage point where she can be seen by everyone, she invites the simple to a feast. Her words are a euphemism for sexual pleasure. "Stolen water is sweet; food eaten in secret is delicious" (Prov 9: 17). Like the serpent in Genesis 3, folly appeals to the forbidden and secretive, presumably vulnerabilities of the young.

Centuries later the erotic appeal of wisdom appears to have prevailed over that of her rival, for Ben Sira has nothing to say about Woman Folly. Although the book is somewhat disjointed, five hymns provide an element of structure to the first half of the book (1:1–10; 4: 11–19; 6: 18–37; 14:20–15: 10; and 24:1–34). The first unit praising wisdom locates all understanding in God and calls wisdom beyond human ken. "The sand of the sea, the drops of rain, the days of eternity," introduce the question: "Who can count them?" The verse is reminiscent of impossible tasks posed by the angel in Second Esdras. In verse 3, Ben Sira continues as follows: "The height of heaven, the breadth of the earth, the abyss, and wisdom – who can search them out?" Only God the truly wise knows the answers to these questions. Wisdom's role is that of a divine agent bringing knowledge to the ignorant.

In 4:11–19, Ben Sira shifts from the relationship between God and wisdom to that of teacher and student. Wisdom's pedagogy includes tests and the possibility of failure. Those who succeed will enjoy YHWH's approval as well as hers, for they have endured the harsh discipline that enables growth. As a reward, they will serve in high places. The third unit, 6:18–37, consists of three stanzas each beginning with "my son" in 6:18, 23, 32, language also found in Proverbs, Egyptian, and Sumerian texts. Relying heavily on agricultural images, it suggests arduous toil and patience while awaiting harvest, the final reward. Verse 22 introduces a wordplay on the name wisdom utilizing the noun *musar* or discipline and the verb sur, to turn aside. In a word, wisdom lives up to her name. The previous fetters are transformed into garments worn by priests and royalty. The hymn concludes with advice to attach oneself to a wise person, visiting him often. This observation may imply a tutorial relationship, which does not accord with Ben Sira's later remark about his school. The ending in verse 37 underscores the theology from Proverbs that associates fear of the Lord and wisdom.

The next eulogy of wisdom in 14:20–15:10 has three themes: the search for wisdom, wisdom's response, and those who choose not to seek her. The successful pursuer will use every opportunity to be near her like a hunter chasing prey. Even a kind of voyeurism is encouraged. The allusion to the children of a pursuer suggests that "my son" and the captions may not imply a young person in Ben Sira's mind. The reference to tent, tree, and fear of YHWH points forward to the crown jewel of these eulogies, 24:1–34, to be discussed later.[29]

While religious people were attempting to bridge the gap between deities and humans, a quite different intellectual quest was being undertaken, one that made the gods more approachable but also introduced the possibility of idolatry.

## 2 God in the Image of Human Beings

Hidden within the first biblical reference to women and men is an audacious claim that they are made in God's image. Granted, being like a deity is considerably less daunting than participating in divinity, having been created from the blood of a god, the claim in the Sumerian creation story *Enuma Elish*. The additional remark in Gen 1:27 that he made them "male and female" is puzzling, coming as it does on the heels of an exalted view of humankind. The

[29] The analysis of Sirach's five hymns about wisdom by Walter T. Wilson, *The Wisdom of Sirach*, ECC (Grand Rapids, MI: Eerdmans, 2023), 43–46, 75–79, 94–100, 183–190, and 274–291 is unsurpassed.

confusion vanishes if the assessment reflects a polytheistic environment with sexual differences among the gods.

The source of the high praise of humans rules out even a hint of pride, for the supposed speaker is Elohim, the general name for God preferred by the priestly author of Gen 1:1–2:4a. This elaborate myth of origins of both the cosmos and its inhabitants inspired the author of Ps 8. Reflecting on the liturgical account of creation, the psalmist fails to mention an image of a deity and its sequel, male and female. Instead, the psalmist imagines human beginnings as observed in nature. The word "suckling" is juxtaposed with a refrain celebrating the excellence of the name Yahweh.

Like Gen 1, the psalmist has a high opinion of humans who are said to be a little lower than Elohim, a word that is capable of several meanings (God, angels, divine beings). In Gen 1 and Ps 8 that possibility includes dominance over animals, birds, and fish. Although the elevation of humankind in Ps 8 comes from a mere mortal, it registers astonishment at YHWH's readiness to look upon the work of his fingers with care.

The Hebrew Bible never mentions the image of God again. The idea does occur in Sir 17:3, but in the context of human mortality. For Ben Sira, the expression seems to imply speech, sight, audition, and cognition, but also the strength that makes possible the dominance over beasts and birds. The emphasis falls on intellectual and ethical qualities in 17:6–7, but the capacity for relationships is implied by an eternal covenant believed to be established by God.

A related idea in Lev 19:2, attributed to God like Gen 1:26, suggests that likeness to deity is something to be acquired by human effort. "You shall be holy as I am holy" is presented as an aspiration rather than a quality already possessed. According to Leviticus, holiness defines the very essence of God, not just external resemblances to mortals. In *An Immense World*, Ed Yong argues that all living nonhuman creatures have evolved over billions of years to maximize their sensory organs and that scholars who fail to take that "sensory bubble" into consideration get things wrong.[30] In other words, if we apply our own sense of sight, sound, touch, taste, balance, and more to nonhuman species, we misunderstand them. Does Yong's warning also apply to every discussion of deity?

The biblical depiction of divinity was informed by discussions in the ancient Near East over more than three millennia. The imagined strength of gods recalled lions or semi-mythical monsters. Such imagination did not exclude relational aspects that humans exhibit, especially speech and emotion. Iconography from

[30] Ed Yong, *An Immense World: How Animal Senses Reveal the Hidden Realms around Us* (New York: Random House, 2022).

the world of the Bible preserves this early stage of reflection on divinity. A mix of nonhuman and human features reveals a desire to combine the known and the unknown. The result is mystery inspiring awe, and relationship encouraging worship.

As civilizations advanced from agrarian to urban living, people viewed gods differently. Images borrowed from nature gave way to royal metaphors. The subsequent decline of the imperial might leaves room for a rise in the importance of the family. With that shift came a more intimate view of God as a parent. Those changes occurred without erasing vestiges of previous understandings. The biblical God's domain expanded, making YHWH lord of the storm, king and father.[31]

One might say that thinking of God as "like humans" is a matter of expediency. Communication requires speech, relationships involve emotions, and activity demands mobility. Human beings from Paleolithic times have imagined a personal relationship with the incomprehensible, whom they depicted in quasi-human form, whether Mother Earth or the Sky God. A spiritual quest with Aristotle's Unmoved Mover or Tillich's Ground of Being would never have occurred to them. There is, however, a danger in making deity like humans: bestowing our own prejudices and longings on the gods. Even when speech, emotions, and mobility are present, they do not necessarily compromise divine hiddenness, at least for the author of Job in 38:41–54.

In Gen 1–11, God is pictured like the gods of Egypt and Mesopotamia. He speaks, rests, walks in the cool of an evening, seeks information, punishes offenders, shows favoritism, has regrets, kills innocents, and fears immigrants from below. It was left to the prophet Hosea to explore the emotional depths of the biblical God. In metaphorical language God is a husband, has an unfaithful wife, has children, divorces the wife, denies paternity, and tries to reignite her ardor (Hos 3). The prophet's agonizing question, attributed to God, "How can I give you up . . . ?" in 11:8 comes from a long cognitive assessment of Israel's infidelity, her preference for a rival god, Baal. The sacrificial system in Israel introduces another kinship between humans and God, for it implies that divine hunger requires sustenance, human or animal.

This kind of talk opens the door for exploring another side of human nature but now attributed to God. It did not take long for those who told stories about God and his dealings with Israelites to introduce instances of divine egoism, frustration, bias, and instability. Perhaps monotheism and a huge ego go hand in hand, for God must be recognized and acknowledged as the only deity. After all,

---

[31] Thorkild Jacobsen, *The Treasures of Darkness* (New Haven: Yale University Press, 1976) detects this shift in Mesopotamian religion.

the search for the number one in intellect, athletics, and love has been around for a long time.

An excellent example in some ways akin to wisdom in its exquisite display of rhetorical questions and repetition is the contest of Darius' pages in I Esdras 3:1–4:4. It aims to prove who is wisest by the answer to the question, "What is strongest?" The answers, wine, king, and women and truth are explored with masterful eloquence. The fruit of the vine overcomes social barriers, destroys family bonds, makes one irrational, and erases memory. Kings, however, reign over everyone else, send men to combat and take their spoils, are obeyed even without having to issue a command, live off the taxes of subjects, and are safe from harm even when sleeping. The third answer, women and truth, devotes the lion's share of time to women. The defense is persuasive, giving the impression that the addition of truth may derive from another source. Women give birth to and clothe those who plant grape vines and to kings. Men go to war and bring the spoil to women, labor to acquire gold or silver but upon seeing a beautiful woman gaze upon her with open mouth and gladly give her the treasure. Men leave father and mother to live with a woman; they even lose their minds over women. As for the king, he easily becomes subject to his favorite concubine, pleading for her favors. Truth, however, is eternal. Everything else dies, even the sun.[32]

The desire to be recognized as number one comes through loud and clear in Isa 40–55. The divine boast in 41:4, "I, the Lord, the first, and with the last; I am He," comes from the one described as creator and sovereign over earthly rulers. God insists that he created the world to be inhabited, an allusion to chaos in Gen 1:2, and that he has no rival ("I am the Lord, and there is no other," 45:18). If true, it means that idols are human artifacts, products of nothing but the imagination, a point that will be made again and again.

Divine frustration as an expression of wrath, the result of a rebellious spirit attributed to the people by one prophet after another, lies behind constant threats and clear disappointment laid bare in prophetic oracles. The impression that the chosen people, according to the biblical perspective, was incapable of goodness, a condition assumed to be the case also with goyim, is voiced in Jer 17:9 ("The heart is deceitful above all things, and desperately corrupt . . . "). The skewed view of human nature gave rise ultimately to liturgical prayers confessing sinful bondage and pleading for its removal.

[32] For analysis of this rhetorical gem, see James L. Crenshaw, "The Contest of Darius' Guards in 1 Esdras 3:11–5:13," 74–88 and 119–120 in Burke O. Long, ed. *Images of Man and God: The Old Testament Short Story in Literary Focus* (Sheffield: Almond Press, 1981), reprinted in *Urgent Advice and Probing Questions,* 222–234.

God's bias permeates the Bible from the favor shown Abel's sacrifice to 2 Chr 36:22 or Mal 4:4–6, the last books in the Hebrew Bible and the Septuagint (Greek translation). This lack of fit with the claim that God created all peoples fails to register sufficiently to bring about a strong dissenting voice. Another perspective is occasionally seen, for example in the story of Ruth, a foreigner drawn into the ancestry of David. Nevertheless, the bias is so strong that even many prophets bought into it (Joel 3:1–8, 19–21).

God's instability as perceived by a devotee causes profound agony in Jeremiah. His accusations stem from extreme disappointment. He believes loyalty has been repaid by something akin to rape. Deceit has replaced truth, making the prophet wish he had never been born (Jer 20:7,14). Ironically, the story of Jonah puts one instance of divine instability in a favorable light. The anticipated bias toward Judah is set aside long enough to spare repentant citizens of Nineveh despite their previous cruelty.

At least one individual in ancient Israel recognized that an uncrossable chasm separated humans and God, rendering useless all such comparisons.

> For my thoughts are not your thoughts, neither are your ways my ways, says the Lord. For as the heavens are higher than the earth, so are my ways higher than your ways, and my thoughts than your thoughts (Isa 55:8–9).

The danger of humanizing God did not escape the poet who put these words in God's mouth. He surrounds this warning with an assurance of divine readiness to pardon, indeed a willingness to come out of hiding. In addition, he compares the faithfulness of the divine word to rain and snow whose effect is to make agriculture, and hence life, possible. That God hides is asserted in Isa 45:15, also in a context of salvation ("O God of Israel, the Savior"). Besides exposing idolatry as a failed enterprise, this securing of divine mystery calls into question every human imitation of deity. According to Exod 3:14, hiddenness extends to the divine name. In short, if true, every word about God is a projection of the human imagination.

Such a conclusion accords with the premise that knowledge derives from observing reality and coming to grips with the options presented to the viewer. However, that perspective was not always operative in wisdom literature which has numerous assumptions about deities that cannot be verified. The sages seem increasingly ready to entertain ideas more at home in Torah and Prophecy (divine speeches in Job, the place of Israel in God's benevolence in Sirach and Wisdom of Solomon). Did this readiness to accept traditional ideas cause Qoheleth to react negatively and raise the possibility of something approximating fate, a kind of ancient karma?

## 3 Act/Consequence or Divine Intervention?

Egyptian wisdom literature and its Sumerian counterpart usually take the form of instruction. Even the alternative form, the simple saying, has a pedagogic intent like instruction. All teaching depends on predictability. It would be senseless to tell someone to adopt character-forming behavior that promotes social solidarity if by doing so one did not reap the desired benefits. Warnings against destructive conduct, too, would fall on deaf ears if by avoiding drunkenness, violent fights, sexual liaisons with married women and so forth, no benefits were forthcoming.

The instructions presuppose a promise that a given action has a predictable consequence. That nexus has been called several things in scholarly treatises: act/consequence, cause/effect, Tun-Ergehen-Zusammenhang, character/consequence, and reward/retribution.[33] The principle behind this connection in Egyptian literature and god's role in assuring that virtue is rewarded, and vice punished have been widely debated. So has the part YHWH played in positive or negative reinforcement of act/consequence in biblical wisdom.

The debate among interpreters concerns whether the wise believed in divine freedom or a mechanistic universe. A royal propaganda myth in Prov 25:2 involves a reciprocal drama in which God hides valuable information about the universe and the king searches for it. That myth is stated differently by Qoheleth. In his democratizing words, God bestowed on all humans a gift but denied access to it (3:11). Its effect, ironically, is to encourage a lifelong intellectual quest. The poem in Job 28 also restricts wisdom to God. All others hear only a rumor about the truth, but their eyes are closed. Knowledge, that is, is only half-knowledge. Ben Sira agrees that the search for wisdom never ends, for he thinks secrecy belongs to Wisdom's name.

Behind this myth is God's freedom to act without restraint from external sources. No order governing the cosmos itself, no cosmic justice established by ma'at, no principle in Mesopotamia called the Tablets of Destiny (ME), no biblical concepts of justice (*mishpat*) and right dealing (*tsedeqah*) can cancel the deity's freedom. The aphorism "Humans propose but God disposes" leaves no doubt that God prevails in competition with royalty, even a king with Solomon's reputation as wiser than anyone else in the East.

A mechanistic understanding of the way things work in human relationships seems to rule out any role of gods. Three things should factor into every

[33] Samuel L. Adams, *Wisdom in Transition: Act and Consequence in Second Temple Instructions* (Leiden: Brill) argues that wisdom was eschatologized because of a political state of anomie. A righteous person's inheritance was no longer gladness, joy, and long life but glory everlasting and peace eternal (237–242).

discussion of this issue. First, no single instruction or saying represents the worldview of the wise. Each one expresses the view of a particular person, place, and time. For this reason, it must be set against other teachings that express a different view of things. Second, there was never a rigid mechanistic view of act/consequence, even if an instruction fails to mention God. Third, the teachings may represent an ideal construal by one sage or by many rather than reality. An important distinction is necessary. "The god" in Egyptian texts does not suggest monotheism; it is rather a sign of respect for other local deities in a polytheistic society.

In Egypt, ma'at was believed to control order or justice (i.e., solidarity, reciprocity, and retribution). To love ma'at is to be socially responsible by behaving in a manner that contributes to harmony and avoids chaos. Such conduct naturally leads to reciprocity, for good treatment of others generates a response in kind. The opposite is also true; abusing others verbally or physically stirs up animosity and foments revengeful acts.

Loving ma'at is a personal choice, not a predetermined cosmic force. Act/consequence is the result of individual motivation rather than a theory of world order. The cardinal virtues in Egypt rest on an ethic that is autonomous and social. They include family affection, honesty, justice, kindness, loyalty, diligence, and moderation. No divine command lies behind these virtues. Self-interest is sufficient motivation for good behavior.[34]

It has been argued that with the New Kingdom Egyptian thought experienced a Copernican shift to personal piety in *Amenemope and Anii*.[35] This much is incontrovertible. *Merikare* asserts that every deed has its consequence ("A blow is repaid by its like; to every action there is a response"). *Anii* thinks of God as a potter and mortals as clay, meaning that God impoverishes if he wishes, and the late Demotic *Papyrus Insinger* teaches that "the fate and fortune that come, it is the god that sends them." Both *Ankhsheshonq* and *Insinger* question the old view that success comes from living right. They seem content to introduce paradoxical formulations in which morality and piety are fused. The turbulent times leading up to their instructions may partially explain this shift in attitude. Thebes fell to Assyria in 663 and Persia defeated Egypt in 525, ruling until 404.

Given the significance of consistency in this literature, it is remarkable that the sages admit their ignorance about the gods. That evidence of intellectual

[34] See Miriam Lichtheim, *Moral Values in Ancient Egypt*. Orbis Biblicus et Orientalis 155 (Göttingen: Vandenhoeck & Ruprecht, 1997), 77–88 and *Maat in Egyptian Autobiographies and Related Studies*. OBO 120 (Göttingen: Vandenhoeck & Ruprecht, 1992), 28–47 and 145–154.

[35] See Rainer Albertz, *Persönliche Frömmigkeit und offizielle Religion: Religionsinterner Pluralismus in Israel und Babylon* (Atlanta, GA: Society of Biblical Literature, 2005), 23–49 and 165–190 for Israel and Babylon.

honesty is widespread. It is found in Mesopotamia in *I Will Praise the Lord of Wisdom* and in *The Babylonian Theodicy* where one speaker calls knowledge of the gods impossible for what appears to be good to humans may be evil to the gods, and the other adds that they endow humans with lies. In Egypt, *Amenemope* admits to an ignorance of the gods, and in biblical wisdom Agur laments the lack of sure knowledge of God. The affirmation of consistency in an uncertain universe has been called the great paradox of wisdom literature. The reason: a great unknown exists between reliable wisdom and what occurs.

In Proverbs, the connection between a deed and its consequence is like that in Egypt. Biblical sages also believed in predictability, but they too recognized that exceptions took place. The admission in Prov 29:13 that God gives luster to the eyes of the poor and the fraudulent leaves the door open for inconsistency, even if some people may have turned a blind eye to it like the author of Ps 37:25. In short, God causes the sun to shine on the just and the unjust. As in Egypt, God's role in Proverbs is unclear. Klaus Koch compared it to that of a midwife, God merely assisting in the process of reward and retribution.[36] Other interpreters have reached a different conclusion; in their view, God carries the act to its consequence. Prov 24:12 supports the latter view, while 11:3 implies an inactive deity. The dominant view seems to be the conventional one, that God intervenes in the process (3:26, 10:3, 21:2, 24:17, 30:6).

With the emergence of personified wisdom as portrayed in Prov 8, God's activity receives an added dimension. It is even said that YHWH decrees wisdom just like the law (2:6). The latest collection, 1–9, adds a theological undergirding, the fear of YHWH. This fragile structure is not sufficient to unite all the collections, but Ben Sira tries to make up for what Proverbs lacks. Even this religious touch does not negate the universal application of wisdom in Proverbs, for Wisdom calls out to all humankind (8:4).

Sometimes the exception to the rule is so extreme that it evokes passionate dissent. That is precisely what the book of Job exposes. His friends illustrate the fallacy of reasoning from external circumstances to personal character. In short, the three friends believe that Job's suffering is a direct result of act/consequence. The poet lays bare the cruelty of such thinking while refusing to depict God as subject to an external force requiring justice in every case. In doing so, the author reveals the psychological and intellectual complexity of every sensible discussion of divine justice.

The author of Ecclesiastes drank from the same fountain that nourished the poet who entertained the possibility that God's justice was unreliable. Qoheleth

[36] Klaus Koch. "Gibt es ein Vergeltungsdogma im Alten Testament," *Zeitschrift für Theologie und Kirche* 52 (1955), 1–42. An English translation can be found in James L. Crenshaw, ed. *Theodicy in the Old Testament* (Philadelphia, PA: Fortress & SPCK, 1983), 57–87.

believes that human destiny is predetermined by something akin to fate and that death cancels all human effort, rendering life empty. While Job's agony was intensified by a strong, personal relationship with God, suddenly broken without cause, Qoheleth was convinced that a remote impersonal deity had replaced the compassionate God portrayed in some texts of the Bible. For him, God's remoteness does not free humans to act as they please, even if it does encourage a paucity of words of supplication (5:2). Examples of a failed connection between act and consequence (8:14) do not rule out divine action. Qoheleth thinks God arbitrarily doles out wisdom and folly as well as strength, punishing in anger (5:6). Irony prevails when Qoheleth says that wisdom, like money, preserves life (7:12). How can it do so when all are caught in death's net like fish or fowl (9:12)?

His pessimism is best seen in 9:13–16, a brief story with irony clinging to every word.[37] There was a tiny village in which a poor but wise man lived (an anomaly in the optimistic world of Proverbs). A powerful king marched against the village, but no one remembered the man who could have saved the people (wisdom is worthless unless it is acted upon). Alternatively, he was consulted, and the village was saved (no one remembered the poor wise man; gratitude for sages is in short supply). The poor man never experienced the immortality promised in an Egyptian text, The *Immortality of Writers*, or even that of a rabbi who quipped ("When the dead are mentioned their lips move").

What has happened to cause the anxiety over death in Job and Ecclesiastes? The sayings in Proverbs and in Egyptian wisdom do not present death as an existential problem. Do Job and Ecclesiastes reflect a less stable society, one where life under foreign rule is subject to rapid change? Or is Qoheleth's interest in death the result of growing philosophical presence?[38] Perhaps the answer is both personal and social, just like the responses to death. As the poet pictures it, the depth of Job's suffering pushed him to wish for vindication beyond death, but in a sober moment he dismisses such false hope. Qoheleth seems content to think of breath returning to its source, but that belief gave no comfort. Ben Sira views death as God's eternal decree (38:21), hence no cause for anxiety (41:1–4). He objects to an idea that was becoming popular in his day, first introduced in the Bible in the second century. That novel belief – those

[37] See James L. Crenshaw, "Poor but Wise: (Qoh 9:13–16)," 153–156 in Susan Ackerman, Charles E. Carter, and Beth Alpert Nakhai, eds. *Celebrate Her for the Fruit of Her Hands: Studies in Honor of Carol L. Meyers* (Winona Lake, IN: Eisenbrauns, 2015) and Crenshaw, *Qoheleth: The Ironic Wink* (Columbia, SC: University of South Carolina Press, 2013).

[38] Peter Machinist, "Fate, *miqreh*, and Reason: Some Reflections on Qoheleth and Biblical Thought," 159–174 in Ziony Zevit, Seymour Gittin, and Michael Sokoloff, eds. *Solving Riddles and Untying Knots: Semitic Studies in Honor of Jonas C. Greenfield* (Winona Lake, IN: Eisenbrauns, 1995).

whose names are written in the Book of Life will awake from the sleep of death to eternal life while others will experience never-ending punishment (Dan 12:2). This concept is found in I Enoch, Wisdom of Solomon, and texts from Qumran.

What did Ben Sira think about act/consequence? His view is close to the one in Proverbs. He denies that anyone who fears the Lord has ever been forsaken by God, a compassionate sovereign (2:10–11; 33:1). Divine mercy lies at the heart of Ben Sira's teaching (51:29; 18:29; 35:20; 2:18, "as his majesty is, so is his mercy"). But that does not rule out wrath (5:6; 16:12), for both good and bad things come from God (11:14). Humans are endowed with the power of inclination; the choice is theirs either to obey or disobey God's commandments (5:14–15). God sees the most hidden sin performed in the dark of night, for his eyes are 10,000 times brighter than the sun (23:19).

In one important respect, Ben Sira moves in an entirely different direction from Proverbs. He introduces traditional beliefs from primeval myths, patriarchal narratives, historical and prophetic books. In these accounts God is viewed as actively directing the Israelites, rewarding them for obedience and punishing them for disobedience. In Ben Sira's view, Abraham obeyed the law of Moses long before it had been revealed, for which God rewarded him. From chapter 44 to the praise of his contemporary High Priest, Simon, in chapter 50, Ben Sira lauds Israel's leaders as divine agents working to advance history in the direction desired by God.

By incorporating this emphasis into wisdom literature, Ben Sira shifted the focus from the individual to the community. In doing so, he added an element wholly at odds with early wisdom: divine favoritism for Israel. That new sentiment permeates the prayer in chapter 36, even to a plea that God lift a hand against foreign nations. In this context, polytheism comes to the forefront. Ben Sira links Israel's well-being with God's sovereignty over other gods (36:5).

The author of Wisdom of Solomon follows Ben Sira in seeing God behind Israel's history but puts more emphasis on Wisdom's role as the earthly manifestation of the transcendent deity. He applies the number seven to this story of divine leadership of the elect just as he did to God's attributes, although multiplied by three. In the context of the assertion that God is the sole deity (12:13), he discusses the distress brought by the worship of idols. In 13:1–16:1, he gives three explanations for this adulation: (1) patriotism, (2) grief over the loss of a loved one, and (3) artistic skill. Those reasonable explanations for idolatry do not prevent him from mocking the futility of praying for safe travel from a statue that is immobile, for life from a dead object, and for health from something weak, to which may be compared Sir 30:19.

While Ben Sira attributed death to the first woman (25:24), Wisdom of Solomon blames it on men who, despairing over life's brevity and finality, chose to crown themselves with rosebuds at others' expense (2:6–20). Alternatively, he thinks death resulted from the devil's envy, but God intended life for humans created in the image of his eternity (2:24). Like Ben Sira, this teacher considers God merciful. In 11:21–12:2, he contrasts God's mercy with the infinitesimal smallness of humans who are like a speck that tips scales, a drop of morning dew on the ground. Grace and mercy belong to the elect (3:9), even if a perishable body weighs down the soul (9:15).

In wisdom literature, God's intervention in human affairs receives more attention in the second century with Ben Sira's conservative return to views more common in other parts of the canon. Pseudo-Solomon pushes this trend even further under strong Hellenistic influence. How did they influence the way God's communication with mortals was viewed?

## 4 Communication across the Eternal Divide

People in the ancient Near East believed that the cosmos had three spheres: heaven, earth, and the underworld. The sun god was thought to have journeyed from heaven, across the orbit of the earth, and through the underworld before returning home. During the third leg of the journey, darkness covered the earth. At death, people went to the abyss, Sheol in the Bible, but unlike Shamash or Re, they never returned. Were the heavens silent except for thunder as in Psalm 29, probably influenced by texts from ancient Ugarit, or did a breaking through the silence of eternity, beautifully proclaimed in Psalm 8, match the turbulence of a storm? The answer to that question differed in monotheism and wisdom. This section examines these differences.

The sun god was not the only one believed to have spent time in the earth's sphere. A convenient explanation for giants, the offspring of gods mating with humans, can be found in the biblical story, a motif familiar to students of the *Iliad* and the *Odyssey*. Did the gods wish to do more than sire children? Did they wish to communicate with humans? To answer that last question, we must look beyond wisdom literature in the ancient world as depicted in other genres. This move alone introduces the problem, at least for sages. Was reason sufficient, or did people require direct or indirect communication from the divine?

A brief episode in the Sumerian story of the first man has the god of wisdom, Ea, communicate by means of a whisper. The intent, however, was to mislead Adapa and thus to prevent him from becoming immortal. Even when the desire is less malicious, as in biblical prophecy, God's reluctance to be fully known may be present. The Hebrew expression, *ne'um 'adonai*, suggests a faint whisper, as if that is all God wishes to convey. Such a desire is surely behind the story about God's refusal to give Moses access to his name. No more than "I am that I am" is freely given. Behind this reluctance is a belief in the power of magic before which even Yahweh exercised caution.

The human desire to control the gods motivated priests to devise any means at their disposal to compel a favorable response. The casting of lots, sacrificing of animals and examination of livers, shooting of arrows, and more reveal the intensity of individuals charged with the responsibility of crossing that eternal divide. Stories about building a tower to heaven, ascending a ladder to heaven, and riding a chariot to the realm of God attest the fascination with bridging the gap from below.

Magic was not the only means of attracting the gods' attention. The other way was through subservience, specifically a bended knee and fervent prayer. For that endeavor, laments provide ample witness, both in the Bible and throughout the ancient Near East. So do liturgical prayers where confessions of guilt abound, along with requests for mercy. Encouragement for this endeavor was found in hints from heaven that the gods wanted to be known by humans even if it meant a degree of lessening the mystery surrounding them.

Theophanies, divine self-manifestation, convey this message while reminding mortals that these precious disclosures come at a cost. Accordingly, they are thought to be accompanied by terrifying cosmic displays of fire, wind, storm, and earthquake. Biblical examples are found in God's appearance to Moses on Mount Sinai, the manifestation in disguise to Elijah, and the divine speeches to Job from a whirlwind. Perhaps the shortened name *Yahu* conceals the human response to a theophany, an ecstatic shout "Oh He." How could one respond other than with a shout expressing awe in the presence of the numinous? One can compare the prayer to Thoth, the god of wisdom ("O Thoth, you well that is sweet to a man who thirsts in the desert. It is sealed to him who finds words, it is open to the silent; comes the silent, he finds the well. To the heated man you are hidden").[39] The silent one is the Egyptian term for a sage, the heated one for a fool.

Another indication that the gods wanted to enter a two-way communication with humans is the phenomenon known as prophecy. Over forty texts from ancient Mari have survived, along with a few from Nineveh, that probably influenced biblical prophecy. Individuals chosen to be spokespersons for the gods understood themselves as messengers delivering the exact words believed to come from a god. In a sense, they spoke as divine mouthpieces. Hence the

[39] Lichtheim, *Ancient Egyptian Literature*. Vol. 2, 114.

introductory phrases, first in Mari, later in the Bible: "Thus has X spoken," "utterance of X," and "the god X has sent me."

Divine communication, however, had to be interpreted, encouragement to heed added, threats as well. Prophets clothed their message in poetry, all the while translating the putative divine words into language common to the hearers. Because competition clings to mortals, rivals eager to curry favor dared to utter an opposing message. Kings seeking authenticity demanded a lock of hair and a piece of a garment from prophets at Mari, presumably to hold messengers accountable for their words. This flaw inherent to prophecy eventually led to its decline, for criteria to distinguish true from false prophecy were never found.[40]

Communication from the gods came in one way that left no room for doubt about its source, at least for those who accepted the prologue to law codes as authentic. Each collection of civil and criminal legislation from Hittites, Assyrians, and Israelites is said to contain direct words of a deity, making it the code binding on all. Hammurabi asserts that Anum and Enlil named him to promote the welfare of the people. The biblical expression "written by the finger of God" pushes the connection between God and law to the limit.

Mortals were not only messengers believed to have been sent from above. Biblical stories of such representatives from another realm suggest that the messengers were thought to resemble humans so closely that their identity as other than mortals was hard to recognize. The result was uncertainty in stories involving Abraham and Samson's father, Manoah. Identity is often cloaked in language implying divinity, as in the story about Jacob wrestling with a mighty opponent. By the time of Jewish pseudepigraphic writings, the skies are virtually filled with messengers called angels, now bearing personal names.

The personification of wisdom discussed earlier is the boldest manifestation of God in the Bible because of its duration and essential connection with the heavenly sphere. With Ben Sira, something entirely new appears. Wisdom is believed to have assumed the role of the spirit in Israel's history. Pseudo-Solomon views her as divine essence on earth, not just *pneuma* but also *logos*, spirit and word. This development is one of the most fascinating transformations in the Bible, for it is largely the fruit of colliding cultures, Jewish and Hellenistic. Ben Sira allows the Judaic traditions to prevail over Greek philosophy, whereas Wisdom of Solomon lets Greek ideas take preeminence.

[40] For discussion of conflict among prophets and the impact of failing to find adequate criteria to distinguish authentic from false prophets, see James L. Crenshaw, *Prophetic Conflict: Its Effect upon Israelite Religion, Beihefte für die Alttestamentliche Wissenschaft* 124 (Berlin: de Gruyter, 1971).

In 7:22–8:1, Pseudo Solomon eulogizes Wisdom in images very much at home in Hellenistic philosophy. Borrowing from cosmology, he credits Wisdom with twenty-one attributes of deity. In his view, she is God's emanation, sharing his essence just as rays of the sun are one with their source. She is God's breath, the very word (*logos*) he speaks. She reflects his light, mirrors his activity, and images his goodness. She is superior to the sun and stars, for darkness overcomes their light. She is ubiquitous, ordering the universe and penetrating all things with wisdom (*Sophia*). His aim with these images is to balance transcendence and immanence. The remote God of monotheism lacked grace and mercy essential to devotees, whereas the immanent God of sages failed as sovereign over all eventualities.

By the time the author wrote these words, God was thought of as more and more distant, possibly because of a chaotic political situation under Ptolemaic and Roman rulers. Even biblical prophecy no longer uses "thus says the Lord" but looks back on the age of direct communication from God. In its place, apocalyptic, a new phenomenon, emerges, one filled with bizarre images, dream-visions, and mysterious numbers to circumvent authorities who looked for any sign of political insurrection.[41] For these revolutionaries, monotheism encouraged division, just the opposite of wisdom, which promoted a stable society.

The Stoic idea the of cosmos as an organic whole with an ordering principle was incompatible with a God who intervened in human affairs the way YHWH is said to have acted. An answer came from Middle Platonism which combined a transcendent principle with an intermediate figure related to both realms. Wisdom was that entity for Wisdom of Solomon. As such, she guided Israel's leaders and the nation itself to a destiny determined by God.

Wisdom's self-praise in Prov 8 evolved over the years into more than a personification. In Sirach, she is the object of praise by a sage who values her equally with the Mosaic law, and in Wisdom of Solomon, she has finally become a divine emanation.

## 5 Evil in Excess, the Flaw in Creation

A transcendent female connecting heaven and earth put additional strain on monotheists already struggling to deal constructively with an increasingly popular rival to God with ruinous intentions and powers. Was there a fundamental flaw in creation?

[41] See the magisterial discussion of counter discourse as resistance to hegemony by Anathea E. Portier-Young, *Apocalpyse against Empire: Theologies of Resistance in Early Judaism* (Grand Rapids, MI: Eerdmans, 2011).

The biblical story of creation goes to great lengths to label the finished product as good, indeed very good. This assessment is attributed to none other than the creator, Elohim. The world we live in is perfect, or so the author of Gen 1:1–2:4a believed. So did the poet who composed Psalm 104. Exuberant praise of God stands out in a book consisting mostly of complaints. The poet surveys creatures beyond humans – lions searching for prey, birds singing in trees and building nests, goats leaping on mountains, rabbits hiding among rocks. For them, God provides water, food, and a place to rest in a safe environment. In this idyllic world, humans are expected to imitate Yahweh by transforming a fixed state into something better – seed into grain, grain into bread, but God supplies basic needs – wine for happiness, oil for a luminous countenance, and bread for strength. The creatures under ships outside human reach leave the poet awestruck over divine benevolence and wisdom.

Foreign influence on the psalm shows deep embeddedness in the environment. The phrase "rider of the clouds" is the Canaanite god Baal's epithet, while "clothed in light" and "messengers of fire" come from Egyptian solar worship. Kinship with *The Hymn to the Aten* goes beyond adoration to specifics, praising the sun god for creating an orderly universe where all creatures can thrive, animate (birds, fish, beasts, and chicks) and inanimate (trees and ships). Both Psalm 104 and *The Hymn to the Aten* manifest deep piety and appreciation for the good earth and its creator.

The more we learn about the origin of the universe today, the greater our awe. That recognition of its grandeur does not move us to ignore the fragility of our tiny part of the cosmos. We remember the Ice Age and fear global warming; we know that asteroids remain a threat; and we understand that our sun will eventually "burn up" or become a dark hole. The ancients may have been awestruck by the cosmos, but they also harbored suspicion that it held fearsome monsters. The texts from Ugarit refer to a water monster with a name like Leviathan in Job. A crocodile-like creature was also feared and worshipped in Egypt, along with a mythic one resembling a hippopotamus. This monster, Behemoth in Job, is called the first or finest of God's creations. Biblical authors differ in their understanding of these monsters. In Job, they seem to be playthings of YHWH but terrors to humans. Other biblical texts tell of God's struggle to overcome these creatures of the deep whose victory would have resulted in chaos (Ps 89:10–11; Isa 25:6–8; Job 38:8–11; and 40:25–32).

For the first humans, threats to daily existence came from many sources: earthquakes, violent storms, floods, fire, disease, and beasts. The danger of childbirth, hinted at in the story of the first disobedience, is coupled with threats from snakes. The additional perils of social interaction, especially war and bondage, make an optimistic assessment of the world almost laughable.

One can argue that adversity builds character and that without challenges virtue never emerges. While the slogan in the sports world, "no pain, no gain," makes some sense, the problem arises when evil in excess makes an appearance. Suddenly the idea that evil is an illusion loses force. What about free will as an explanation for extreme evil? That argument covers only a small percentage of human suffering, for it ignores societal constraints, intellectual limits, and psychological ambiguities. Free will implies choice, but in many circumstances, individuals have limited freedom, if any at all.

For some people, as for Dostoevsky, the suffering of innocent children tips the scale away from a well-ordered universe to a flawed one. They ask: "How can a loving God remain idle while innocent children suffer and die from disease and warfare?" Who can find comfort in the explanation by Pseudo-Solomon that a prescient God took children early, knowing that they would commit a grievous offense if allowed to live long enough to do so? When religion promises well-being to the worshipper, but events expose the lie, an explanation is needed. Hence theodicy. That is precisely what happened in the world of the Bible, and the literature is rich beyond measure. Like the search for criteria to distinguish true from false prophecy, the responses to theodicy offer no satisfactory answer. They do, however, highlight a flaw in the universe.

For modern secularists who benefit from the insights of Copernican astronomy, Darwinian biology, Freudian metapsychology, Marxist ideology, technocratic cultural biases, higher biblical criticism, unjust distribution of human resources, mass atrocity, and calamitous natural events, the easiest response is to deny the existence of God. Recent dogmatic atheism has come to rival fundamentalism in its claim to represent absolute truth. Ancients did not consider atheism a possibility; the closest they came to it was practical atheism, living as if God did not matter in their lives. Such atheism is rare in the Bible, although it would hardly appear in a text focused on securing divine favor. Those who dared to deny the existence of deity risked being called fools as in Psalms 10 and 14 or liars as seems to be the case in Prov 30:1–14.

Roads to practical atheism vary. Psalm 10 appears to suggest that God's failure to investigate and punish evildoers implies his nonexistence. Wholesale corruption leads the author of Ps 14 to accuse perpetrators of thinking there is no God. Proverbs 30:1–14 advocates theoretical atheism while ironically confessing ignorance about mythic images and God. The devout ending requires an about-face unless it is part of a debate between a theist and an atheist.

Blaming evil on one of the many gods believed to fill the heavens was easier than practical atheism. That exclusionary approach left one's special god free of guilt for the wrongs on earth. Widespread belief in divine councils was an inference from royal courts on earth. It was left to the author of Ps 82 to help bring about an ethical transformation of polytheism to monotheism and in doing so to render theodicy more urgent than before. The psalmist imagines God standing to judge in the divine council and pronouncing the gods guilty for failing to assist orphans, the poor, and the weak. The striking parallel with a Canaanite text can hardly be missed, for there the prince Yassib demands that his father Keret relinquish the throne for failing to attend to the needs of widows and orphans. For his temerity, Yassib pays a high price. In Ps 82 the punishment for the offense is death. Immortal gods are said to become mortal due to an ethical shortcoming. An ironical ending declares the biblical God guilty too. Such is the implication of the fervent appeal that Elohim come to the aid of the distressed.

Biblical stories about demonic figures offer another response to theodicy. Bad things can be blamed on them, letting God off the hook for injustice. As we have seen, tales involving demons expose a dark side of God unless they can be attributed to lesser beings like rebels who have fallen from heaven or vicious messengers from above who pose as divine. Often the stories leave the identity of an assailant unclear, possibly a reflection of authorial discomfort over their content. Unlike ancients who believed in demons, moderns find such talk bizarre like polytheism, and for many, monotheism also. Resorting to semi-polytheism at the expense of lesser gods fails at theodicy, for these lesser beings exist at the indulgence of higher gods.

From the moment of creation, the Bible describes a world order in which God endows humans with free choice, holding them responsible for the consequences of decisions. The price of human freedom is divine constraint resulting in a clash between God's sovereignty and free choice on the part of humans. The result is God's vulnerability, necessary in every intimate relationship. The covenant that makes relationships possible exposes God's pathos, a capacity to love deeply but also vulnerability to extreme suffering.

The exercise of free choice introduces a clash between individual and corporate solidarity, for one person's decisions frequently affect others' well-being. The cycle of sin, punishment, repentance, and deliverance in the Deuteronomistic history reflects the dominance of corporate solidarity in early Israel, whereas Ezekiel 18 indicates a shift toward individual responsibility. The mood behind the proverb cited by Jeremiah and Ezekiel, "Our fathers have eaten sour grapes and the children's teeth are set on edge," shows the extent of resentment over the idea of transgenerational guilt and punishment.

Ezekiel's rhetorical strategy in attacking the ideas expressed in proverbial form reveals the power of realism in his audience. He imagines someone objecting ("Yet you say" and "God is unfair"). The prophet's defense of divine justice on the individual level would fail in any court. Evidence supporting the unnamed speakers can be found on every street and behind closed doors. Ironically, the choice by a sovereign to remain aloof while injustice happens frees the deity from a charge of manipulating human events, but it identifies God as unjust.

Divine sovereignty and free choice by humans are irreconcilable, clashing like justice and mercy. Can limited divine power and knowledge, essential for human freedom, support theodicy if one distinguishes between potential and actual divine attributes? In other words, God has absolute power and knowledge but chooses not to use them. Failing to actualize both results in injustice. One need only think of the Holocaust, Hiroshima and Nagasaki, and countless other atrocities that make theism a difficult worldview.

Can a split personality explain God's failure to actualize potential, voluntarily suspended to permit free choice? By God's admission to Moses, conflicting attributes make up the divine essence. Although God chooses to emphasize mercy, it comes at the expense of justice. That is the force of the closing remark about punishing future generations for ancestors' sins (Exod 34:6–7). The story of two sojourners assuming the role of judge illustrates the absurdity of someone pronouncing judgment who comes from an alien worldview and lacks authority (Gen 18:25; 19:9). To save innocent people in Sodom and Gomorrah, Abraham dares to ask, "Shall not the judge of all the earth do right?" His nephew Lot, spared because of Abraham's courage and expertise at striking a bargain, even with God, is accused of acting as judge over citizens of a doomed Sodom. Together these episodes provide a perfect paradigm of theodicy, for humans are quintessentially sojourners. Ancient Near Eastern sojourners who complain to deities about injustice are less direct than Abraham, who stands before God as dust and ashes but nonetheless challenges the deity.

Jeremiah pushes beyond questions to bold confrontation when accusing God of seduction and rape, a convenient metaphor for betrayal (20:7a). He does the unthinkable – reading an indictment against God (12:1–2). It was left to Jonah to highlight the irreconcilability of divine justice and mercy. A reluctant and disobedient prophet becomes a recipient of divine mercy only to be piqued when God extends mercy to hated Ninevites, suddenly repentant. God's question to an angry prophet suggests that he has learned from Abraham ("Should I not have compassion on Nineveh . . . (4:11)?" The literary form, parody or satire, cloaks the issue under discussion, defining it for popular consumption).

Whereas Jonah chose to indict God's compassion, Joel implores it after an infestation of locusts threatened the entire population, provoking the thought of a final day of judgment. Innocent people are nevertheless urged to turn to God in repentance, but Joel can only echo Jonah's "Who knows whether he may turn and relent?" (2:14). Just as Jonah appealed to the confessional creed in Exod 34:6–7, Joel calls God merciful, compassionate, patient, and loyal. How could people under such peril believe in divine compassion? The change from compassion to wrath had come at God's own choosing. We see here the strong impulse to resist any thought that God changes (cf. Mal 3:6a,7b).

A moment's reflection on parental guidance leads to another response to theodicy. Discipline within the home promotes character formation and protects inexperienced youth from harm. Ancient Israelites viewed God as a loving father reluctantly punishing children for disobedience. The prophet Amos recites a history of recurring sins despite God's attempts to turn the people around through timely discipline (Amos 4:6–11). A fivefold refrain sets off this liturgy with the words "Yet you did not return to me'," leading to a final threat. It is unspecified, but the words "Prepare to meet your God, Israel," leave no doubt about its nature.

Less direct but infinitely more intimate, Hosea's example of divine discipline is set within the context of a loving father teaching a child to walk and soothing hurts. A change of images introduces the notion of care for oxen involving a yoke. Loving care did not prevent Israel from serving Baals and provoking divine wrath. Hosea imagines a struggle within God's soul over whether to abandon his beloved or to use a more serious type of discipline, one that ends in exile (Hos 11:1–7).

Israel's sages also emphasized God's parental discipline but introduced an intermediary female whose erotic appeal lessened the pain from her yoke. In Ben Sira's eyes, her harshness eased as students began to submit readily to her demands. Pseudo-Solomon applied Wisdom's corrective discipline to historiography, and like Ben Sira broke away from the individualism of earlier teachers.

Reward and retribution, the most common response to theodicy and potentially the cruelest, comforts religious people who imagine God seeing every good deed and rewarding in a commensurate manner. While retribution instills fear in some, punishment often falls on innocents. The imaginary world behind much of the Bible fails to correspond to reality, for in the real world neither reward nor retribution is always operative.

The classic exception to belief in exact reward and retribution is Job, who is considered righteous by the narrator and God, but who is thoroughly wicked in his friends' eyes. What else could they think, given the widespread belief in reward for virtue and punishment for vice? Israel's historiographers, priests, and prophets pushed that view to the limit, as did sages and Psalmists. The author of Psalm 37 claims to have lived to old age without seeing the righteous forsaken or their children begging for bread (v 25).

Behind this view is an assumption that the universe operates on a rational system that hands out reward and punishment relative to an individual's merit. That assumption is grounded in a deep psychological need for order. Fear that chaos has the upper hand is allayed in God's promise to Noah that he will never again lash out in a way that threatens human survival. In some Eastern cultures reward and punishment is extended into several lifetimes.

The tenacity of the retributive view rests on the fact that it works in many cases. The exceptions are the problem, for they bring extreme agony to some people. An example from the story of Gilgamesh is illustrative. When the gods kill his companion Enkidu because Gilgamesh had slain the guard of a forest, Gilgamesh cries out: "O my brother, my dear brother! Me they would clear at the expense of my brother."[42] In his mind, punishment should fall on the guilty.

When things go awry between humans and God, someone must restore harmony or chaos reigns. In the ancient world, two theological systems emerged. In one, the guilty individual was responsible for making things right; in the other, an innocent person paid the price of atonement. Both systems depended on a just God. Individual merit was dominant in the Bible, and even substitutionary atonement required a personal act of repentance to make it work.

A gnawing sense of guilt accompanied misfortune in the ancient Near East. Prophets, priests, and sages in Israel believed sin was widespread but they refused to blame it on God (Sir 15:11–12). Although God was thought to hate sin, he looked with compassion on sinners. Occasionally, however, punishment fell on an innocent, as in the story of David and Bathsheba. Even prayer could not save the infant conceived in an adulterous act (2 Sam 12:14). An innocent substitute paid for their sin, violating the supposed principle of merit. The sacrificial system, probably borrowed from the Canaanites, allowed for an animal to take upon itself the sins of the people.

In the sixth century, a prophet introduced a novel theory of vicarious atonement involving a righteous servant who bore the sins of many (Isa 52:13–53:12). Early Christians applied this idea to Jesus, and the identity of the servant has been widely debated. The most likely victim was either King Josiah or the nation Israel. The radical idea that innocent suffering benefits others was taken over by some rabbis despite its centrality to Christians.

For many, the most satisfactory response to theodicy is to extend reward and punishment beyond the grave. Belief in survival after death has been traced to Paleolithic and Neolithic times. Two rival views developed, one among seminomadic wanderers, and the other among city dwellers in Mesopotamia. The first involves the belief that the dead rested in their

[42] Pritchard, *Ancient Near Eastern Texts Relating to the Old Testament,* 86.

graves as “living corpses.” This view is found in Gen 3:19 and Eccles 12:7 in the expression “dust to dust” and “breath to its source.” The most widespread view was that the dead are shades in tempestuous waters called Sheol. According to both views, no one ever returned for permanent residence.

A breakthrough occurred in ancient Israel based on two things: passionate communion with God and a conviction that there was no limit to God’s power. The Egyptian *ba* was matched by belief in an immortal soul, and the conviction that nothing could separate humans from God evoked the belief that God has swallowed death forever (Isa 25:8). Legends about Enoch and Elijah being taken into heaven circulated and psalmists spoke of deliverance from Sheol (Ps 49:16) and like Enoch being received in honor (Ps 73:24). The clearest statement of life beyond the grave appears in an addition to the book of Isaiah (“Your dead will live, their corpses will rise,” 26:19a). Martyrdom intensified this belief (Dan 12:1–3; 2 Mac 7:1–42), one staunchly resisted in some circles (Job, Qoheleth, Sirach).

Intellectual honesty requires every response to theodicy to be labeled uncertain. The biblical characterization of God as an active player in the human drama is a result of writers who appear to know God’s innermost thoughts, despite belief that the deity is hiding. They would, in all probability, have insisted that their description of God is not subject to rational investigation. All human knowledge is necessarily partial when viewed from the perspective of divine mystery. That is the insight proclaimed in Job 28, and it applies to every response to theodicy.

Qoheleth agrees with the author of Job 28 that knowledge of God is limited but, like Job, he adopts an agnostic position. In his view, God has withdrawn, and humans cannot know anything about his actions. Ironically, that agnosticism did not prevent him from any number of assertions about divine activity. The glaring inconsistency is also found in the book of Job where his friends’ conventional wisdom has more than equal voice to Job’s unorthodox views.

For many people, the best response to theodicy is that of the grammarian and philosopher Saadia Gaon. God has bestowed on us the greatest gift possible: life. Beyond that, God owes humans nothing, which rules out arguments based on merit. For more than 5,000 years people have tried to justify the ways of gods or a God. They have spread the blame around at the expense of lesser deities or demons. They have redefined God by stressing limitations of divine power and knowledge or a split personality. Alternatively, they have viewed evil as discipline and, less helpful, punishment for sin. Finally, they have shifted to the human scene, viewing suffering as atonement and banking on life beyond the grave.[43] The whole venture has failed because of partial human knowledge and the mystery surrounding the deity. All talk about God is a product of human imagination, which changes as cultures advance and mix. Is anything permanent? What about the universe?

## 6 Divine Decree and Cosmic Order

For law, the second pillar of monotheism, to be absolute, it must come from a source other than human. Case law varied with location and circumstance. That is why emperors like Hammurabi claimed to present divine statutes to their subjects. Sages, however, believed that lessons learned over generations sufficed to face reality. The tension between these opposing views never disappeared entirely, even if eased by linking divine law with the harmony of the created order.

The complicated relationship between law and wisdom is on display in Sirach. Although the two are flip sides of a coin, Ben Sira makes the matter even more confusing by speaking of law in three distinct ways. He sees law as the Torah, that is, the content of the first five books of the Bible. He also thinks of law as parental instruction, just as sages in the book of Proverbs understand the Hebrew word *torah*. Finally, he views law as individual mandates from God that cover all aspects of life. Pseudo-Solomon emphasizes the two sides of a coin, namely ethos and case law.

This view of customary behavior and law dates from Israel's tribal state when a *beth 'ab* (family) was presided over by a patriarch, otherwise known as a paterfamilias. A group of families comprised a clan, and the larger unit was a tribe. In those early days mothers and grandmothers with good memories preserved insights based on customary behavior, while elder men gathered data on things like oxen that gored or sexual transgressions within a close-knit family. Over time this collection of data was solidified as custom (or propriety) and law. The former depended on consensus while the latter was enforced by tribal elders who met at city gates and rendered decisions. That task was eventually taken over by the state.

Both custom and law allowed for exceptions. For example, anyone guilty of a revenge killing could flee to one of the refuge cities set aside for sanctuary, and even the *lex talionis* – an eye for an eye – was adapted to circumstances. In Israel the concept was a humanitarian move to prevent excessive cruelty like

[43] For extensive discussion of these responses to theodicy, see James L. Crenshaw, *Defending God: Biblical Responses to the Problem of Evil* (Oxford: University Press, 2005). See also Antti Laato and Johannes C. de Moor, eds. *Theodicy in the World of the Bible* (Leiden: Brill, 2003).

Lamech's oath to exact seventy-seven-fold revenge (Gen 4:24). Occasionally, Israel differed from her neighbors in matters like the punishment for adultery, for no monetary compensation was permitted. The code of hospitality so essential to nomadic life was extended to include sojourners in Israel, whereas non-biblical references mention only widows, orphans, and the poor in contexts of the hospitality code.

Several law codes in written form have survived from the ancient Near East. The best known is that of *Hammurabi*, but it was preceded by *Ur-Nammu*, *Lipit Ishtar*, *Eshnuenna*, and two codes from the Hittite kingdom. These law codes were thought to have been decreed by the god of each nation (e.g., Marduk, Ishtar, and so forth). The law of Moses is said to replace the tablets broken in a moment of rage over the people's crafting and worshipping a golden bull. Biblical law is unique in that it is set within a historical context and is based on a covenantal relationship. It is assumed that Israel agreed to subject itself to divine rule. Personal choice is therefore not ruled out. Later rabbis tell an amusing story about God offering the ten commandments to other nations, all of whom turned down the gift because living in accord with its mandates would require them to give up so much pleasure. The irony of this self-congratulatory tale did not escape those voicing it, for the biblical stories about Israel's own failure to obey divine law are widespread, leading to confessional prayers in beautiful liturgies.

Law and ethos are the glue holding society together. They represent two approaches to reality. Law was believed to derive from divine decree, a revelatory act. Ethos, however, was a human achievement consistent with a decree of cosmic order at creation like that attributed to the Egyptian goddess ma'at. Ethos depends on consistency or reliability; a good deed must result in reciprocity else consensus will not develop. Wickedness results in punishment, according to this principle.

Ben Sira's appreciation for cosmic order may have been based on Stoic philosophy, but it could have derived from Psalm 104 and the glowing praise attributed to heavenly beings in the book of Job. In one way Ben Sira goes beyond those expressions of awe, for he comes close to mathematical precision in praising the universe for its splendor and magnificence. He would be at home with some modern astronomers who think the timing of every stage in the evolution of the universe rules out a theory of accident or randomness.[44] Some sceptics reluctantly concede that lack of randomness demands a creator.

[44] See Stephen Wong, *Creation: Science?* (North Point, Hong Kong: Paper House, 2023), 113–141 for an assessment of randomness in the evolution of the universe.

In a single lifetime, numerous examples of discord seem to throw a question mark over belief in cosmic order. Ben Sira drew on psychology to defend traditional belief, one grounded in Stoic philosophy. He recognized that everyone has nightmares, but he claimed that the wicked are plagued sevenfold (40:1–11). Their yoke is unlike that worn temporarily by Wisdom's devotees, for it lasts from womb to womb, by which he means from birth to death when one resides in Mother Earth.

Sayings and instructions in the book of Proverbs seldom take a psychological approach to things, probing the inner self and its profound inclinations. The closest they come to the unconscious *id* and *ego* is a wry comment that "the heart knows its own bitterness, and no stranger shares its joy" (14:10) or "even in laughter the heart is sad, and the end of joy is grief" (14:13). That realistic view is reminiscent of Qoheleth, who thinks of dreams as the result of excessive activity and talk (5:3,7). Job's friend Eliphas describes a nocturnal visit by a spirit that brought a message from God in the form of a question. "Can a mortal be more righteous than the Maker?" (4:12–21), a slightly veiled attack on Job who is by all accounts in the Prologue completely faultless. As for Job, he considers dreams instances of divine malfeasance, for which he wants God tried and found guilty. Elihu, however, thinks dreams and visions open human ears, enabling sinners to return from their evil ways. Visions, that is, are a form of discipline, a view close to that of Ben Sira.

Anxiety over dreams has a long history. Wisdom literature from Mesopotamia involved magic and specialists' interpretation of the configurations in livers. The court stories of Joseph and Daniel that tap into mantic wisdom attribute the secret knowledge to YHWH. The dreams and visions in the book of Daniel are matched by their prominence in Pseudepigraphic wisdom literature, which must be viewed against the background of apocalyptic, where frightful creatures, images, and numbers represent various nations and kings. The epithet "Ancient of Days" first appears in this literature.

Qoheleth places the thought of death at the center of his teachings, bringing them to an end with a remarkable poem about the debilitating process of old age and its finality, the return of the breath to its source. Ben Sira links concern over death with lack of sleep, confusion, and troublesome visions that amount to nothing. He mentions a specific nightmare from which one awakes – fear brought on by having escaped from combat. Anxiety may strike the king and pauper, according to him, but the wicked experience a host of dangers which he names one by one. They include death, bloodshed, strife, sword, calamities, famine, affliction, and plague. One might call the dreams to which he refers "nightmares for the wicked," proof that in the words of a country music song "Your cheating heart will tell on you." The impression Ben Sira gives is that cosmic order operates unfailingly. He does concede that virtuous people may experience minor inconvenience, but the wicked bear the lion's share of grief (40:1–11). Observations like these are unfounded deductions from traditional orthodoxy at odds with reality. In developing this psychological response to theodicy Ben Sira draws heavily on prophecy and historiography miles apart from previous sapiential teachings.

What did Pseudo Solomon think about dreams? Living in Alexandria, the intellectual capital of the world, he was enthralled by Hellenistic philosophy. At the same time, he surely admired vivid apocalyptic images for their realism in depicting human anxiety. With a divided audience, Jews and Egyptians, he tried to maintain a balance when rewriting the story of Israel's escape from slavery. He must have known that no record of Joseph or the death of a whole generation of Egyptian first-born children had survived in Egyptian literature. Nor was there any written account of the supposed events except the biblical one composed to magnify YHWH at Pharaoh's and his god's expense. A moment's reflection would have convinced him that the story about his ancestors' slavery in Egypt could not bear scrutiny.

Perhaps the worship of idols was a phenomenon worthy of study, for the learned among Egyptians would consider adoration of an object that could not avoid bird droppings mere superstition. He chose to concentrate on the stupidity of worshipping a thing crafted by artists rather than the Creator of all artifacts in their unfinished state. In 17:1–21, he takes up Ben Sira's psychological argument and exposes the folly that brought disaster to Egyptians. In doing so, he thinks nature has turned against idolatrous Egyptians while the same natural elements nourished Israelites. Finding no rest in inner chambers, they imagined specters, phantoms, dismaying faces, and delusions. Trapped in a prison not made of iron, these miserable people called on magicians and the wise among them for help, to no avail. The paralysis, he insists, was self-inflicted, an inner fire like Jeremiah's agony over perceived betrayal by YHWH.

In 18:5–19, Pseudo-Solomon rehearses the story of Israel's escape from bondage with minor casualties and Egypt's sore affliction, but with one striking addition reminiscent of Rev 19:13. The all-powerful word leaped from heaven and touched heaven while standing on earth. The result: apparitions in dreadful dreams and death all around. John's fertile imagination sees heaven opened and a white horse ridden by one called Faithful and True, but also the Word of God. In each case, the heavenly visitor is called the divine word (*logos*), another name of Wisdom.

Pseudo-Solomon boasts about his full knowledge of the structure of the universe, something taught him by Wisdom (8:17–22). That fund of knowledge included times and seasons, what Qoheleth describes in a poem that has been called a Stoic insert (3–1–9). For cosmic order to benefit humans, individuals must be able to align their lives to this order. The problem, as Qoheleth sees it, is that no one knows the proper time for these important moments. Wisdom enables us to approximate the time to plant, for example, but conditions beyond our control may affect the maturation of the seedling. That same uncertainty applies to the other times, leading him to ask: "What gain has the worker from his toil?" (3:9).

Qoheleth did not think it possible to benefit from God's gift, which he calls *'lm* in 3:11. The Hebrew word is capable of two meanings depending on the vowels assigned to the consonants. If one reads *'olam*, it implies something like "unto the ages," perhaps a sense of eternity. Alternatively, a reading of *'elem* suggests something secretive, a thing beyond discovery. The immediate context favors the latter interpretation, for it cannot be found. The words "from beginning to end," however, are more in line with the former meaning. One may want to join Qoheleth in asking: Who knows? For him that means nobody.[45]

In this section, we have observed important changes in the sages' understanding of ethos and law. Whereas custom arose as individuals explored ways to cope with daily situations, it later became subservience to God and to the order provided by Providence. Law, too, changed from statutes by which subjects proved their loyalty to their Sovereign to a divine emanation variously named *Hokmah, Sophia,* and *Logos*. Has God also changed?

## 7 An Evolving Concept of Deity

A reasonable person will admit that our understanding of God has changed over millennia. During the long period that our ancestors hunted for food, mostly from animals stronger than them, but also from nuts, grain, and fruit, they thought of God as a spirit in various elements of nature, especially trees, rocks, and wind. Once they became agriculturalists and domesticated animals, they formed city-states and the strong among them imposed their will on all. In a sort of politico-morphism, they began to look upon God as supreme ruler over empires. When empire after empire fell to a stronger force, the will of the people, families emerged as central to social solidarity. With that change, the parental role of educator was thrust into the limelight. Moreover, views of God became more intimate without any lessening of divine sovereignty. Three metaphors cover the different stages: spirit, king, and father.

Behind this shift in metaphors historians of religion detect progress from animism, the belief in embodied souls, to polytheism, monolatry, henotheism,

[45] See James L. Crenshaw, "The Eternal Gospel (Ecclesiastes 3:11)," 548–572 in *Urgent Advice and Probing Questions.*

and monotheism. If we can imagine god indwelling a tree, why can't we think of many gods, each of whom fills a need in our lives? But who likes to share the limelight? Surely not gods. So, we begin to think of one supreme being and multiple lesser gods. The next stage is to worship one God but believe that others exist, even if they are not very important to you. The final step is to deny the existence to every god but one, which inaugurates a problem: explaining evil. Hence dualism, monotheism's byproduct.

Wisdom changes just as our view of God does. The five biblical books usually classified as wisdom literature reveal distinct concepts of deity. From creator and guarantor of providence in Proverbs to malevolent fiend indifferent to human morality in Job, to something akin to fate called chance in Qoheleth, to a more traditional mix of historiography, prophecy, and priestly teachings and earlier ideas from Proverbs in Sirach and Wisdom of Solomon.

Christian theologians, too, have changed with the times, the most radical one resulting from the Enlightenment and Darwin. Trinitarian orthodoxy gave way to more rational views of religion. Heavy emphasis on history evoked a reaction characterized as romanticism which gave way to neo-orthodoxy with resonances of saving history, ultimately to non-revelatory sapiential, interdisciplinary, and literary emphasis more in line with the interests of scholars in departments of religious studies. Perhaps the biggest change is the way Israel's beginnings are viewed. The exodus from Egypt is seen by many as fiction and the Israelites are thought to have been settlers in the hill country who broke away from Canaanite masters and took with them worship of Baal, elements of a language, and much more.

Those who do not accept historical criticism as a heuristic aid to understanding the Bible probably agree that changes have taken place as described, but they still adhere to a traditional approach that, in their words, takes sacred scripture literally. For them, the Bible is the inspired word of God and true from beginning to end. Some traditionalists recognize the problematic nature of such a claim. To resolve the difficulty, they presume an original perfect text, one that has been lost beyond discovery. The Isaiah scroll from Qumran makes that argument dubious, for it coincides with the Masoretic Text in all essentials.

This evolution within theological discourse has been replicated in the scholarship of individuals. Gerhard von Rad, perhaps the most influential biblical interpreter in the twentieth century, began his career stressing little historical credos that cited YHWH's actions directing the nation Israel by means of divinely appointed leaders. Like most interpreters at the time, he considered wisdom literature irrelevant because it did not extol YHWH's saving deeds in history. Despite his self-description as "a little historical monoman," von Rad came to emphasize God as a creator. In his thinking, God's work in nature replaced a historical emphasis. With that shift, divine silence trumped revelation, and wisdom literature claimed his attention.[46]

Four recent publications about God reveal additional changes in how the deity is viewed by the larger public. Karen Armstrong, *A History of God,*[47] discusses the theological dance between revelation and reason over five millennia. The three Abrahamic religions, Judaism, Christianity, and Islam, represent faith based on revelation. Vedic religions, Buddhism and Hinduism, see faith as humans transcending reason and ascending into the depths of the self, an act without the need of direct contact from the gods. Armstrong's magisterial analysis of the struggle to keep God sufficiently personal to interest humans and transcendent enough to attract worshippers does not overlook the mystical alternative in every religion.

She does not mince words about her negative view of YHWH, who, in her eyes, replaced a mild deity, El, and became an "irascible, despotic, brutal, partial, and murderous god, YHWH Sebaoth." The hostility toward other gods displayed by his followers was a new phenomenon, she thinks, as was the marginalization of women that accompanied the rise of cities and aggressive capitalism in the Axial Age. Nor does she fail to recognize the peril that trinitarian theology in Christianity presents to monotheism, even if Hinduism had its own version of the trinity in Brahman, Shiva, and Vishnu. Her perceptive treatment of Greek Orthodox theologians and mystics of all faiths illustrates the importance of the creative disciplines like art, music, and poetry as a corrective to extreme intellectualism. In her words, "Where the God of the more dogmatic religions divides humanity into warring camps, the God of the mystics is a unifying force."[48] Meister Eckhart's words, "Man's last and highest parting is when, for God's sake, he takes leave of God," become prophetic in the death of God movement announced by Nietzsche. According to Armstrong, in mysticism there is happiness, ecstasy, rather than breast-beating or remorse, so prevalent in the Reformers, when obsession with Hell was dominant.

She thinks Pascal was the first modern who saw belief in God as a personal choice, for prior to him nobody had seriously questioned the existence of God. The Jewish grammarian and philosopher Saadia, for example, saw doubt, not faith, as needing to be defended. People like Newton, however, did not need to mention the Bible in his General Scholium where he deduces all God's

[46] See James L. Crenshaw, *Gerhard von Rad* (Waco, TX: Word Books, 1978).

[47] (New York: Ballantine Books, 1993). She analyzes the creative imagination behind theological arguments over the centuries, showing the many problems facing monotheism. Its origin is equally complex. According to Laato and de Moor, "The origin of YHWH monotheism is one of the most intricate problems in Old Testament scholarship (*Theodicy in the World of the Bible,* viii-ix)."

[48] Armstrong, *A History of God,* 239.

attributes from his intelligence and power. What happens when humans like Pierre-Simon de Laplace see no need for the hypothesis of God? Her answer: The individual or the Holy Land, as in Zionism, becomes an idol.

If there is a God-shaped hole in the human consciousness, as Jean-Paul Sartre said, what can replace the missing presence? Armstrong seems to hold out a tiny ray of hope, for, she writes, "Human beings cannot endure emptiness and desolation; they will fill the vacuum by creating a new focus of meaning."[49]

The possibilities are endless, but the usual idols of money, power, and fame cannot fill that emptiness. The vacuum requires an explanation for the wonders of the universe that leave one in awe and for the sense of obligation toward one's neighbor that has produced institutions for healing the sick and educating the unlearned through music, art, poetry, and literature of all kinds. Moreover, replacing the emptiness enables the recipient of life and its benefits to express gratitude for this precious gift. The benefits of combatting self-centeredness with adoration of true goodness in a supreme being are priceless. In the words of a noted philosopher, "If there is no God, humans will have to create one."

According to Jack Miles, an esteemed literary critic and journalist trained in biblical studies, God is a deeply flawed fictional character who began as a great communicator but eventually withdrew into silence (*God, a Biography*).[50] Miles arrived at this conclusion by studying the Hebrew Bible in the order of its books. In his view, God creates the human scene by talking to himself. He hopes to change humankind into his image and constantly complains until he is defeated by Job. Silenced, he incorporates a demon into himself, letting humans assume the divine role with the assistance of angels.

What are the major insights from following the flow of the Bible? Until the flood, God is maximally powerful and minimally kind; in the story of Joseph, he is maximally kind and minimally powerful. Uniquely dependent on a human antagonist, God attempts to make humans like him. This is the only plot of the Bible. In it, God is a warrior, and the Bible is about victory. Mutual irritability, God's and humankind's, is the seed of prophecy in which God complains about Israel's complaints. Prophecy is God's self-manifestation, agony, and crisis. By forgiving endlessly, he masters justice and destroys the covenant. God will not make that mistake twice; hence he tries apocalyptic, where God is as disappointed in his people as they are in him.

In Psalms, God's presence and absence rules, in Proverbs, his simple absence, and in Job, the sound of silence. God's rival in Proverbs is not other gods but laws and their equivalents. Wisdom is God's wife or mankind's mother. The book of Job is a profoundly blasphemous story about God. In it might makes

[49] Ibid., 399. [50] Jack Miles, *God, a Biography* (New York: Vintage Books, 1995).

right; justice and power make him God. This God tortures Job by silence; Job's near silence leaves God in silence and agony. Qoheleth challenges hidden promises of monotheism by quasi-Platonic divine foreknowledge of recurring cyclic events. Thoroughly secular, he does not think God very important. In Daniel, God's Bible replaces the Bible's God and angels do God's bidding. The Bible ends with God trapped in himself, like Hamlet.

What does Miles think about monotheism? He writes that "Monotheism's boast is that ultimate reality lives in its house and nowhere else. Monotheism's sorrow is that everything must be accommodated in that one house."[51] That sorrow includes divine irritability, genocide, and egocentricity but also incomprehensibility. Modern readers may rightly ask: "Why did ancient authors imagine such a deity?". We must not forget, however, that sublime teachings attributed to Yahweh have informed the conscience of contemporary humans.

The beauty of Miles' pioneer work is that it emphasizes the Bible as a human product, the result of creative imagination. As such, it encompasses the best and worst humans are capable of thinking and doing. Even the deity they created does not escape the messiness of emotion and its consequences, but the same God also soars to heights imagined by lesser beings but never reached in real life. The unflattering picture of YHWH's journey from speech to mutism underscores a danger in teaching unsavory parts of the Hebrew Bible to children and throws into question the claim that it is divinely inspired. Critics may fault Miles for ignoring the actual history of composition, but he can respond that the approach taken is purely literary. None can deny its accuracy as a literary analysis.

*The Evolution of God*[52] by an eminent evolutionary psychologist, Robert Wright, is every bit as sweeping and provocative as Miles's book. Wright looks at primordial religions in chiefdoms and ancient states as a background for studying the three Abrahamic religions. He discusses early Israel's polytheism, the shift to monolatry, and the emergence of monotheism, topping that off with a look at Philo, a first-century philosopher who spoke of the triumph of *logos*/wisdom. Wright concludes with a discussion of the invention of Christianity, the triumph of Islam, and the moral imagination's global outreach.

The thesis of the book is that humans have created God in their image, and it is now time to de-anthropologize or dehumanize this fictional being. Wright does not say that a reality lies out there, but he does see an equivalence in arguments for God and for electrons, religion and science. God is, he thinks, the

[51] *God: A Biography,* 216. His observations about human nature are often profound. He writes: "In the presence of the truly great, the good always seem small. In the presence of the truly good, the great always seem vain." (284).

[52] Robert Wright, *The Evolution of God* (New York: Little, Brown & Company, 2009).

source of all creativity, the force driving morality and thus essential to humanity. One might call God, in his words, the conscience of the universe.

Wright sees a paradox in that gods arose as an illusion and their history is an illusion, one that points to something like divinity and in doing so has become more plausible. He highlights the human qualities of gods like Inanna, Ishtar, and Enlil who were obsessed with sex but notes that even in Mesopotamia with nearly 2,000 named gods a moral compass emerged, partly because of reciprocal reliance among states. Nevertheless, he writes, divine will was the formal justification for war.

Wright agrees that the pyramid of powers in Mesopotamia and Egypt was a step toward monotheism. The process as he sees it is political. Marduk rose to power with the support of Hammurabi, and in Egypt, Akhenaten did the same by a coup, elevated Re over Amun, and erased the names of gods in some texts. Like many revolutionaries, Akhenaten misread the mood of his time. The fate of his innovation demonstrates the instability of society. What does Wright say about ancient Israel? The people worshipped a warrior God, YHWH, which partly explains the belligerent intolerance of the three Abrahamic faiths. As warrior, YHWH left the task of running the universe to other gods. One can assume that YHWH was originally El or Elyon, rising to supreme God through upward mobility as in Ps 82. Did he have a sex life? Wright's answer: "Maybe he did."[53] He is clearly associated with Athirat or Asherah in some biblical texts as well as extrabiblical ones at Kuntillet 'Azrud and Khirbet 'el-Qom.[54] The fall of Jerusalem in 586 helped monotheism arise, for the people in exile refused to believe that their God had been defeated. Their answer: God was punishing them for sin. With Deutero-Isaiah, a monotheistic impulse emerges. True monotheism awaited the Greek philosophers tired of the sorry behavior of gods in the *Iliad* and the *Odyssey*.

*God, a Human History* by Reza Aslan,[55] an historian of religion, traces the concept of God from its beginnings in the Paleolithic Age to the eighth-century CE Sufi Ibn al-Arabi, who combined the teachings of the poet Rumi, Shams, and Bayazid. In their view, God is the total of all existence, and therefore we are God. Aslan discusses early evidence of worship across the globe, especially the Volp Caves in the Pyrenees where a picture of a man portrayed as a hybrid

---

[53] Robert Wright, *The Evolution of God* (New York: Little, Brown, 2009), 119.

[54] See David Penchansky, *Twilight Gods: Polytheism in the Hebrew Bible* (Louisville, KY: Westminster John Knox, 2005), 75–89 for a helpful analysis of the archaeological evidence from the two sites, as well as that from Elephantine. He argues convincingly that monotheism never captured the hearts of all Israelites. His evidence: the incident of YHWH's defeat in battle by Chemosh, *miqreh,* which he calls "happenstance," the divine council, polemic against idols, the goddess *hokmah,* Lady Zion, and Asherah.

[55] Reza Aslan, *God, a Human History* (New York: Random House, 2017).

animal represents an embodied soul.[56] Named "The Sorcerer," it dates between 18,000 and 16,000 years ago. Another example, Cueva de las Manos in Sante Cruz, Argentina, dates from 15,000 to 11,000 BCE. The paintings of human hands in remote parts of a cave are evidence of worship. From fourth millennium Egypt an ivory and flint knife depicts the lord of beasts, and Neanderthal stone rings in Aveyron, France, indicate early worship.

A clear example of belief in disembodied souls comes from near Urfu in Turkey, Goebekli Tepe, an early Stonehenge (12,000–10,000 BCE). It has stone pillars with human hands and a belt carved into stone. The sanctuary would have taken many workers years to complete. How is God viewed on this site? As a lofty person.

Aslan discusses the humanizing of God in the Sumerian legend of *Atrahasis*.[57] According to it, the gods grew tired of agricultural labor and Enlil consulted Mami, who created humans from blood and clay, putting them to work providing food for the gods. Twelve hundred years passed and the noise from all the people prevented Enlil from sleeping. He called for a divine assembly and by vote it was decided to send a flood. However, a pious man, Atrahasis, was conversant with the god of wisdom, Enki, who told him to dismantle his house and build a boat, taking his wife and kin to safety. After the flood subsided, Atrahasis offered a sacrifice, Enlil smelled it, grew angry, and asked how anyone could have survived. Enki admitted guilt, Mami regretted her decision to destroy those she had created, and a solution was found. Lions, wolves, famine, war, and plague would keep the population under control. Enki then immortalized Atrahasis and his wife. The story is adapted by the Babylonians in the *Gilgamesh Epic* (twelfth century) and by the biblical story of the flood.

In Aslan's view, neither Egyptian nor biblical monotheism endured. Christianity replaced one God with three. With the eleventh-century Iranian Zarathustra Spitama, monotheism and dualism are paired. In a river Zarathustra experienced an epiphany of Ahura Mazda, the God first and last. Zarathustra concluded that this God created everything positive with a negative byproduct. Good can't exist without evil, just as light requires dark. Monotheism and dualism coexist. True monotheism, Aslan thinks, is the legacy of the Sufi Ibn al-Arabi. God is all in all, and we need not fear God, for he exists in our essence. In short, God is human, and the history of God is really that of humankind.

Aslan relies heavily on recent biblical scholarship about the origin of YHWH worship. In short, it began in the Sinai/Paran/Edom/Teiman region, moved to

---

[56] Aslam conjectures that belief in the soul led to belief in God (*God: A Human History,* 47).

[57] See Hallo, *The Context of Scripture,* 450–452.

the highlands of Canaan and merged with El worship. A revolt against Canaanite neighbors in the valley below resulted in two kingdoms, Israel in the north, and Judah in the south. The YHWH worshippers took with them aspects of Canaanite religion, a language, and a culture. Elohim was the preferred name for God in Ephraim, and priestly writers merged El and YHWH, but the names of Canaanite gods Baal, Mot, Yamm, and Shemesh were kept as non-divine concepts. With the fall of Samaria to Assyria in 722, YHWH survived as the god in Judah. Occasionally, YHWH El is combined with Elyon (God most High), *'Olam* (Eternal God), *'Emet* (God of Truth), *neqamot* (*God of vengeance*), and *Ely* (my God).

How did monotheism emerge from henotheism? Primarily through innovative centralization of national worship in Jerusalem which encouraged worship of a single deity and devalued local manifestations. The royal unification of national life was both political and religious. The second known attempt at monotheism was made possible by Cyrus king of Persia, for when exiled Jews returned to Judah, they faced religious life without a sanctuary and needing to explain YHWH's defeat. The answer: YHWH was punishing them for sin.

Following some Egyptologists, Aslan suggests alternative readings of Israelite history in two instances. He writes that the Israelite religion may be a form of Atenism that survived the purge by Tutankamun and that the name "I am that I am" comes from the sun god Re's self-description. Aslan also thinks the episode of the golden calf may be an attempt by Israelites to return to the worship of Hathor, the goddess of motherhood and love.

The views expressed by these four scholars demonstrate the struggle over millennia to grasp two incompatibles: revelation and reason. They raise the question: Do projections of human attributes into the heavens reflect anything more than wishful thinking? They dispute monotheism's assumption of communication between heaven and earth, and they emphasize wisdom's elevation of the intellect while still attempting to explain the long history of seeking meaning in a tempestuous universe.

## Conclusion: The Impact of Monotheism on Sages

One can imagine the reluctance of monotheism and wisdom to leave the womb in which they were warm and secure. A difficult journey awaited each, an adventure in which opposition would be strong. For monotheism, the task was to convince potential worshippers that all their needs would be met by a sole deity. The list of necessities was endless, but the main items included health, prosperity, social status, and longevity. The problem was that a host of rivals vied for providing each of these. The goal facing the newborn: to replace all opposition and assume the task of meeting every need known by supplication. The irony: by assuming responsibility for humankind, the sovereign of the universe also took on the onus for bad things that inevitably befell the unfortunate. At these moments, monotheism may wish to have someone to blame for so many disturbing realities.

Wisdom's emergence from the womb placed her in an equally unpleasant environment. The clamor of voices from prophets and priests claiming divine authority echoed through every hill and valley, drowning out her observations based on nothing but sight and sound. The task she faced was to authenticate conclusions by appealing to the evidence available to every individual who dared to use intellect as sole guide of conduct and conviction. She, too, found the task beyond her ability, and the restraint of reason left room for the humility of prayer. With that tiny crack in her armor came an intermediary from heaven, and this fascinating figure brought with her features that earlier sages had dismissed as nonessential.

Monotheism's byproduct, dualism, emerged early, partly to soften the effects of a transcendental High God cloaked in mystery, but also as a means of shifting blame for evil to lesser beings. If polytheism thrived, there was no need for a scapegoat. Once a god achieved sufficient upward mobility to incorporate the powers of all rivals, the need to explain evil became acute. As the sole deity and ruler of the entire universe, God grew more mysterious. One result was to imagine aid from above in the form of a personified female with extraordinary credentials, for paradoxically the hiding God wished to be known. This magnificent *Hokmah* brought divine wisdom to humankind. The book of Proverbs gives her an erotic rival called Folly, but she appears in no other sapiential text, ancient Near Eastern or biblical.

The figure who brought dualism into the realm of discourse was believed by the prophets Isaiah and Ezekiel to have originated in heaven and fallen to earth as punishment for rebelling against the supreme authority. His biblical credentials are mixed, for in the book of Job he seems to be an emissary of God whose mission is to ascertain the true motive for righteousness. His motto seems to be summed up in a single Hebrew word: *hinnam* (for nothing, without cause). Genuine goodness, that is, needs neither a carrot nor a stick. At first, without a name, he is soon endowed with that dignity and considerably more. As Satan, he becomes a formidable rival to YHWH.

Biblical wisdom is based on experience open to the naked eye. That rule should exclude all talk about God who by nature is invisible, at least to humans. How is it, then, that sages discuss transcendent beings as if they are everyday companions? They imagine God in their own image, just the reverse of the biblical claim that Elohim made humans in the divine image. The problem with this approach to theology is that bad attributes are applied to God along with good qualities. In the end, God becomes an unreliable superman. Nevertheless, the principle of similitude enables humans to think of deity as personal rather than a spirit or Ground of Being. Interestingly, the Hebrew Bible never refers to the image of God again, perhaps because the priestly creation story was composed later than much of the scripture.

Experience taught sages that the universe was dependable despite a few hiccups. The sun god may have struggled mightily to defeat the nocturnal god Apophis, but with dawn came a new day. Reliability in many areas led sages to posit an orderly universe under divine surveillance. That assumption meant that a given act produced a predictable consequence, at least most of the time. It was not clear to the sages whether a god intervened in that process. At times it seems that an invisible principle of act/consequence governed the process from deed to result, but at other times it appears that a god brought reward or punishment. This belief was buttressed by the hope that all ruptures in the scheme of reward and retribution would be made right in a postmortem judgment. The Egyptian *Book of the Dead* gave readers some guidelines about that final assessment of human achievements and failures. In the Bible, this hope of a future reckoning was slow in coming but quickly captured imaginations once it arrived. Sages like Qoheleth accepted the idea of recurring cycles but considered chance more determinative in daily affairs. Neither Ben Sira nor Pseudo Solomon subscribed to his pessimism. For them, divine agents (*Hokmah*, *Pneuma*, and *Logos*} carried out God's will on earth, at least for the favored people.

With the ascendance of monotheism in the Bible came an unwelcome sense of divine absence. Perhaps one of the vestiges of polytheism was a longing for a "handy god." Having a god at one's disposal, as it were, was replaced by a distant deity with a full plate, especially complaints from devotees. Laments from Mesopotamia and biblical Psalms reveal a dissatisfied clientele. Non-sapiential books in the Bible bring worshipper and God closer together through law and prophecy, while at the same time exposing humans to expectations often beyond their ability. Job and Qoheleth considered the absence of God oppressive or indifferent, while the two sapiential books in the Apocrypha emphasize cosmic order like the Stoic concept. Both Ben Sira and Pseudo-Solomon balanced divine absence with the active presence of Wisdom, God's word and law (Ben Sira), an emanation (Pseudo-Solomon). This new development came at a price – universalism wanes as particularism enters biblical sapiential texts.

It has been said that the presence of evil makes any talk about God nonsensical, for the Triad of power, justice, and evil always clashes. If God is all-powerful, evil in excess should not exist. If God is just, how can there be evil?

No one can deny the existence of evil, but God's existence can be questioned. Theodicy goes back as far as the third millennium in the ancient Near East. The literature describes ten different responses to theodicy, all of which appear in the Bible. They range from atheism to an acknowledgment of ignorance, and much in between. They imagine a split personality in God, the impossible attempt to balance justice and mercy. They shift responsibility for evil to a lesser being, or they insist on reward and retribution, if not in this life, at least in another existence. They think of atonement, even a vicarious clearing of the slate, and they take comfort in the mystery of holiness that no human intellect can penetrate. Theodicy has a companion, anthropodicy, for human behavior, too, leaves much to be desired. Who will defend the cruelty that has dogged humanity?

Ethos, the domain of wisdom, resulted from human effort to make sense of reality and bring about individual well-being. Law, however, had to be enforced by authorities; together ethos and law were the glue keeping chaos at bay. At first, they were thought to be two sides of a coin, but the sages responsible for Sirach and Wisdom of Solomon viewed them as separate entities, cosmic order and divine decree. For them, human effort fell to God's initiative just like law. Wisdom changed from a personification of sagacity to a primordial being sent from heaven to assist Israel. As an emanation of God, she brought transcendence to humankind.

Views 'of God have changed over millennia. Not surprisingly, change is ongoing, as can be seen in recent histories of God. In one, an eminent scholar of religion discusses the theological dance involving the struggle to keep together transcendence and immanence, the attempt to give equal weight to reason and revelation. Her global interest makes room for comparison with Vedic religions and the essential role of mysticism. In another, a prominent literary critic depicts God as a fictional character like Falstaff. Following the development of this literary construct in the Hebrew Bible book by book, he emphasizes the deeply flawed deity, a result of creating God in the image of humankind. An evolutionary psychologist traces the view of God from paleolithic times to the present. In his view, God is the conscience of the universe. A historian of religion discusses age-old cave drawings in the Pyrenees, handprints in Argentinian caves, and stone pillars with human hands and belts in Turkey. These all demonstrate the inclination to worship a god who resembles humans. His conclusion, based on Sufi mysticism, is that we are God.

The belief in God has existed since Paleolithic times when humans journeyed underground at considerable risk to worship at a place they considered holy. It appears that people have always inquired about beginnings and endings, the meaning of life and death, the source of evil and reality of good, the consequence of sin and the possibility of forgiveness. A concept of God dominates and enriches each of these inquiries. While the answers, and questions, they have introduced are numerous, the intellectual rigor and enthusiasm show that Augustine was right about the restlessness of many people, and possibly also about the source of rest. Monotheism and wisdom are an uneasy pair, but life would be impoverished without them.

From ancient times to the Common Era, the period covered in this book, sages held ever-changing views of God and wisdom. Beginning in animism, belief in holiness became paradoxically more anthropomorphic and universal, human and transcendent. Wisdom also underwent major changes. Being good was no longer rewarded, and hard toil brought no profit. As social conditions changed, sages became less pessimistic and incorporated aspects of revelation into their teachings. Has God also evolved? The answer is an emphatic “yes” if by God one means the human concept of the Source of everything.

This investigation of the relationship between monotheism and wisdom in the Hebrew Bible resembles the modern controversy over religion and science. The problem has been around for millennia. Just as the modern struggle has yielded no resolution, at least for many people, that engaged in by biblical sages sought unsuccessfully to bring together two incompatible concepts, monotheism and wisdom, an uneasy pair.

# Select Bibliography


Ackerman, Susan, Charles E. Carter, and Beth Alpert Nakhai, eds. *Celebrate her for the Fruit of her Hands: Studies in Honor of Carol L. Meyers*. Winona Lake, IN: Eisenbrauns, 2015.

Adams, Samuel L. *Wisdom in Transition: Act and Consequence in Second Temple Instructions*. Leiden: Brill, 2008.

Albertz, Rainer. *Persönliche Frömmigkeit und offiziele Religion: Religionsinterner Pluralismus in Israel und Babylon*. Atlanta, GA: Society of Biblical Literature, 2005.

Alster, Bendt. *Wisdom in Ancient Sumer*. Bethesda, MD: CDL, 2005.

Armstrong, Karen. *A History of God*. New York: Ballantine Books, 1993.

Aslam, Reza. *God: A Human History*. New York: Random House, 2017.

Armstrong, Karen. *A History of God*. New York: Ballantine Books, 1993.

Barmash, Pamela, ed. *The Oxford Handbook of Biblical Law*. Oxford: Oxford University Press, 2019.

Bergmann, Michael, Michael J. Murray, and Michael C. Ray, eds. *Divine Evil? The Moral Character of the God of Abraham*. Oxford: Oxford University Press, 2011.

Bledsoe, Seth. "Ahiqar and Other Legendary Sages," 267–285 in Samuel L. Adams and Matthew Goff, eds. *The Wiley Blackwell Companion to Wisdom Literature*. London: Wiley Blackwell, 2020.

Brown, William P. *Character in Crisis: A Fresh Approach to the Wisdom Literature of the Old Testament*. Grand Rapids, MI: Eerdmans, 1991.

*Wisdom's Wonder: Character, Creation, and Crisis in the Bible's Wisdom Literature*. Grand Rapids, MI: Eerdmans, 2014.

Buccellati, Giorgio. "Wisdom and Not: The Case of Mesopotamia," *Journal of the American Oriental Society* 101 (1981), 35–47.

Chestnutt, Randall D. "Wisdom of Solomon," 104–121 in Samuel L. Adams and Matthew Goff, eds. *The Wiley Blackwell Companion to Wisdom Literature*. London: Wiley Blackwell, 2020.

Crenshaw, James L. *Defending God: Biblical Responses to the Problem of Evil*. New York: Oxford University Press, 2005.

*Education in Ancient Israel: Across the Deadening Silence*. ABRL. New York: Doubleday, 1998.

*Gerhard von Rad*. Waco, TX: Word Books, 1978.

"Method in Determining Wisdom Influence upon 'Historical' Literature," *Journal of Biblical Literature* 88 (1969), 129–142.

*Old Testament Wisdom: An Introduction.* 3rd ed. Louisville, KY: Westminster John Knox, 2010.

"Poor but Wise (Qoh 9:13–16)," 153–166 in Susan Ackerman, Charles Carter, and Beth Alpert Nakhai, eds. *Celebrate Her for the Fruit of Her Hands: Studies in Honor of Carol L. Meyers*. Winoma Lake, IN: Eisenbrauns, 2015.

"The Eternal Gospel (Ecclesiastes 3:11)" 548–572 in *Urgent Advice and Probing Questions*. Macon, GA: Mercer University Press, 1995.

*Prophetic Conflict: Its Effect upon Israelite Religion*. Beihefte Zeitschrift für die Alttestamentliche Wissenschaft 124. Berlin: De Gruyter, 1971.

*Qoheleth*: *The Ironic Wink*. Columbia, SC: The University of South Carolina Press, 2013.

"The Contest of Darius' Guards in I Esdras 3:11–5:13," 74–88, 119–120 in Burke O. Long, ed. *Images of Man and God: The Old Testament Short Story in Literary Focus*. Sheffield: Almond Press, 1981.

*Theodicy in the Old Testament*. Minneapolis, MN: Fortress, 1981.

*Urgent Advice and Probing Questions: Collected Writings on Old Testament Wisdom*. Macon, GA: Mercer University Press, 1995.

"*Wisdom in Israel*, by Gerhard von Rad," *Religious Studies Review* 2 (1976), 6–12.

Foster, Benjamin R. *Before the Muses: An Anthology of Akkadian Literature*. 2nd ed. Bethesda, MD: CDL, 1996.

Goff, Matthew J. *Discerning Wisdom: The Sapiential Literature of the Dead Sea Scrolls*. *VTS* 116. Leiden: Brill, 2007.

Gregory, Bradley C. "Ben Sira/Sirach," 87–108 in Samuel L. Adams and Matthew Goff, eds. *The Wiley Blackwell Companion to Wisdom Literature*. London: Wiley Blackwell, 2020.

Hallo, William, ed. *The Context of Scripture: Canonical Compositions from the Biblical World*. Vol. 1. Leiden: Brill, 2003.

Hamilton, Victor. "Satan," *Anchor Bible Dictionary*, Vol. 5. New York: Doubleday, 1992, 185–189.

Jacobsen, Thorkild. *Treasures of Darkness*. New Haven: Yale University Press, 1976.

*The Hearts that Once . . . Sumerian Poetry in Translation*. New Haven, CT: Yale University Press, 1987.

Koch, Klaus. "Gibt es ein Vergeltungsdogma im Alten Testament?" *Zeitschrift für Theologie und Kirche* 52 (1955), 1–42.

Laato, Antti and de Moor, Johannes C. eds. *Theodicy in the World of the Bible*. Leiden: Brill, 2003.

Lambert, Wilfred G. *Babylonian Wisdom Literature*. Oxford: Clarendon, 1960.

Lichtheim, Miriam. *Ancient Egyptian Literature*, Vols. 1–3. Berkeley: University of California Press. 1973, 1976, 1980.

Long, Burke O., ed. *Images of Man and God: The Old Testament Short Story in Literary Focus*. Sheffield: Almond Press, 1981.

Machinist, Peter. "Fate, m*iqreh*, and Reason: Some Reflections on Qoheleth and Biblical Thought," 159–174 in Ziony Zevit, Seymour Gittin, and Michael Sokoloff, eds. *Solving Riddles and Semitic Studies in Honor of Jonas C. Greenfield*. Winona Lake, IN: Eisenbrauns, 1995.

Miles, Jack. *God: A Biography*. New York: Vintage Books, 1995.

Penchansky, David. *Twilight Gods: Polytheism in the Hebrew Bible*. Louisville, KY: Westminster John Knox, 2005.

Portier-Young, Anathea E. *Apocalypse against Empire: Theologies of Resistance in Early Judaism*. Grand Rapids, MI: Eerdmans, 2011.

Rad, Gerhard von. *Weisheit in Israel*. Neukirchen/Vluyn: Neukirchener, 1970.

Samet, Nili. "Mesopotamian Wisdom," 328–348 in Samuel L. Adams and Matthew Goff, eds. *The Wiley Blackwell Companion to Wisdom Literature*. London: Wiley Blackwell, 2020.

Sandoval, Timothy J. "The Orality of Wisdom Literature," 267–285 in Samuel L. Adams and Matthew Goff, eds. *The Wiley Blackwell Companion to Wisdom Literature*. London: Wiley Blackwell, 2020.

Schroer, Silvia. *Wisdom Has Built her House*. Collegeville, MN: Liturgical, 2000.

Seibert, Eric A. *Disturbing Divine Behavior: Troubling Old Testament Images of God*. Minneapolis, MN: Fortress Press, 2009.

Sinnot, Alice M. *The Personification of Wisdom*. SOTSM. Aldershot: Ashgate, 2005.

Smith, Mark S. *God in Translation: Deities in Cross-Cultural Discourse in the Biblical World*. Grand Rapids, MI: Eerdmans, 2010.

Uusimaki, Elisa. "Wisdom Texts from the Dead Sea Scrolls," 122–138 in Samuel L. Adams and Matthew Goff, eds. *The Wiley Blackwell Companion to Wisdom Literature*. London: Wiley Blackwell, 2020.

Westermann, Claus. *Roots of Wisdom: The Oldest Proverbs of Israel and Other Peoples*. Louisville, KY: Westminster John Knox, 2005.

Wilson, Walter T. *Ancient Wisdom*. Grand Rapids, MI: Eerdmans, 2023.

*The Wisdom of Sirach*. Grand Rapids, MI: Eerdmans, 2023.

Wong, Stephen. *Creation: Science?* North Point, Hong Kong: Paper House, 2023.

Wright, Robert. *The Evolution of God*. New York: Little, Brown, 2009.

Yong, Ed. *An Immense World: How Animal Senses Reveal the Hidden Realms around Us*. New York: Random House, 2022.

Cambridge Elements

# Religion and Monotheism

---



---

## About the Series

This Cambridge Element series publishes original concise volumes on monotheism and its significance. Monotheism has occupied inquirers since the time of the Biblical patriarch, and it continues to attract interdisciplinary academic work today. Engaging, current, and concise, the Elements benefit teachers, researched, and advanced students in religious studies, Biblical studies, theology, philosophy of religion, and related fields.

## Cambridge Elements

# Religion and Monotheism

### Elements in the Series

*Monotheism and Narrative Development of the Divine Character in the Hebrew Bible*
Mark McEntire

*God and Being*
Nathan Lyons

*Monotheism and Divine Aggression*
Collin Cornell

*Jewish Monotheism and Slavery*
Catherine Hezser

*Open Theism*
Alan R. Rhoda

*African Philosophy of Religion and Western Monotheism*
Kirk Lougheed, Motsamai Molefe and Thaddeus Metz

*Monotheism and Pluralism*
Rachel S. Mikva

*The Abrahamic Vernacular*
Rebecca Scharbach Wollenberg

*Monotheism and Fundamentalism: Prevalence, Potential, and Resilience*
Rik Peels

*Emotions and Monotheism*
John Corrigan

*Monotheism and Peacebuilding*
John D Brewer

*Monotheism and Wisdom in the Hebrew Bible: An Uneasy Pair?*
James L. Crenshaw

A full series listing is available at: www.cambridge.org/er&m

For EU product safety concerns, contact us at Calle de José Abascal, 56–1°, 28003 Madrid, Spain or eugpsr@cambridge.org.

www.ingramcontent.com/pod-product-compliance
Ingram Content Group UK Ltd.
Pitfield, Milton Keynes, MK11 3LW, UK
UKHW022143080726
473066UK00010B/728

* 9 7 8 1 0 0 9 4 9 1 8 9 1 *